To Jim :-
    Our love and prayers.
go with you as you
respond to God's calling
to pastor a new flock.

        Nettie & Art Elias

The Last Word

The Last Word

(published and unpublished)

For Christians—and others who take themselves too seriously

by

Jamie Buckingham

LOGOS INTERNATIONAL
PLAINFIELD, NEW JERSEY

The Last Word
Copyright © 1978 by Logos International
All Rights Reserved
Printed in the United States of America
International Standard Book Number: 0-88270-303-X
Library of Congress Catalog Number: 78-56932
Published by Logos International
Plainfield, NJ 07060

To my wife
Jackie
who never has the last word

Table of Contents

Foreword. . .

(Do not read if you are easily offended)

Some books are written all at once. You just go in the room, close the door, sit down beside your barrel of notes and write until the book is done. I've written books like that and it's a lot of fun.

Other books are written, page by page, over great periods of time. These books are interrupted by millions of things. Getting up from your typewriter to change a bicycle tire and not getting back for five days. Rushing upstairs to find out what all the screaming is about. Spending two days in bed because you ate a gallon and a half of ice cream following an argument with your wife. Going overseas for three weeks to see if things are still okay in the Orient. Spending an entire afternoon holding up that little floating bulb in the back of an overflowing toilet while your wife looks for the misplaced pliers so you can shut off the water. Wasting an entire evening looking for your glasses and getting so frustrated you throw papers all over the floor, which takes all the next morning to straighten out. Leaping up from your chair and rushing out to see what the loud explosion was in the garage. And crouching under the windowsill in the living room until the group of angry women from the church finally stop ringing the doorbell and disappear down the front walk.

This book is like that. It took seven years to write. It, too, has been a lot of fun.

It all started when we moved back to Florida. My old friend John Schumann, editor of the *Vero Beach Press Journal* (who didn't know I had become a religious fanatic) asked me to write a weekly editorial page column "on any subject."

That's like turning a hungry dog loose in a meat market. You see, I see God in everything—and sometimes newspaper editors wish I didn't. Six months later, however, when John S. tried to drop my column from the paper, he found it had become more popular than his boring editorials. He couldn't get rid of me.

But that didn't make him wish he couldn't, however. There was the time the real estate people in our little Florida town threatened the newspaper with a class action suit over something I had written. Then the automobile dealers took great exception to my column on what it was like to buy a new car and threatened to withdraw all advertising unless I was fired. Twice, over the years, the local ministers wrote letters of protest. Especially were they upset when I urged all my readers to show up at church the next Sunday with tambourines. On one occasion, after I had written a column about conditions in Appalachia, a group of Kentucky coal miners threatened to come to Florida and burn down the editor's house.

The editor, frustrated, finally went berserk. He rushed into the composing room and, according to witnesses, with shrieks of wild laughter, erased all the hair off the picture which ran with my column. (This came after a number of readers wrote saying the picture I was using with my column was twenty-four years old and I had grown bald in my old age.)

The next issue, in a column about spiritual hypocrisy, I pointed out that old John S. had been importing California oranges to eat for breakfast. Of course that led to a cross-burning in front of the newspaper office which opened up a wealth of things to write about over the next few weeks.

While all this has been going on at the newspaper, I have also been writing a column for our church paper, *The Trumpet*. Invariably, however, even when I don't want to, I stir folks up. One Sunday morning after church I saw a group of people out on the lawn, their faces red, teeth gnashing, shouting at my wife. She was equally angry, shouting back at them. Finally the group stormed off in all directions and I asked Jackie what was going on. She said they were angry over last week's column in *The Trumpet.*

I thanked her for defending me.

"I wasn't defending you," she shot back, "I was agreeing with them."

Not satisfied with offending the people in my home town and the people in my church, I began writing a regular column for the now defunct Christian newspaper, the *National Courier.* In fact, there are still isolated pockets of people across the nation (and some in the publishing house as well) who believe my columns were the major cause in defuncting that worthy project.

They may be right. I once wrote a column about preachers who smoke and we lost two hundred thirty-eight subscriptions. One preacher sent the editor an envelope full of cigar ashes (which he spilled all over his soup-stained suit when he opened it) to let him know what he thought of a bum like me. Another time I complained about violence in the movies and illustrated it by telling of a violent movie I had seen. This time the paper got angry letters from those who called me a prude for condemning violence, as well as from a number of prudes who canceled their subscriptions because the paper had a columnist who attended violent movies.

There are times when I believe I am the only person in the world who isn't angry.

Recently I sat down and made a list of all the people I have offended over the last several years.

They include:
   bald people
   fat people
   loud-mouthed preachers
   preachers who don't speak loud enough
   women who wear a lot of goop on their face
   men who wear wigs
   people who don't work

people who don't do anything but work
hypocrites
pharisees
pentecostals
Baptists
Catholics
Jews
Arabs
charismatics
holy people
unholy people
my wife
my mother
my wife's relatives
my relatives
and once even my old dog Randy rose up from his favorite place in front of the refrigerator and growled at me.

To my knowledge the only writing I have done which has not offended a lot of people has been the column I've done for *Logos Journal,* "The Last Word." So, even though this book contains a lot of stuff from all these other columns, I've decided to call it *The Last Word* since that is least offensive to most of my readers.

As it says somewhere on the dust jacket (unless some angry editor has scratched it out) this book contains stuff which has been published and stuff which is unpublished.

The published stuff has appeared in these newspapers and magazines I've talked about.

The unpublished stuff hasn't appeared anywhere.

Until now.

Jamie Buckingham
May 1978

The Last Word

1. Things That Go Squish in the Night

One of the advantages of living in the country is the quietness.

One of the disadvantages is having to fool with the water system. I used to complain, when we had our house in the subdivision, about the cost and taste of Florida water. But now, after having moved out into the country—and becoming an expert on wells, pumps, aerators, pressure tanks and water softeners—I'm not so sure I wasn't better off when all I did was turn on the faucet and pay the bill.

Our particular system works from a deep, constantly flowing well. The same well serves the house, sprinkling system and air conditioning / heating units. After flowing through all the contraptions in a pump house in the back yard, the water finally arrives at where we live. The majority of this is drunk, flushed, spilled or used for washing. The rest is piped through the heating units and out through a drainpipe into a pond in the pasture.

To give the system a certain romance, the mad plumber

1

installed a number of secret valves. If these are not opened and closed at critical times the water overflows into the yard, or backs up into the bathrooms, where it does exciting things.

One of these secret valves is connected to the drainpipe going from the heating units to the pond. It is located in the back yard at the edge of the pasture under the barbed wire fence. In case I want to divert this ever-running stream, and use it to wash the car, I only have to turn the valve and open a spigot.

There is one major problem. The cut-off valve which diverts the water from pond to spigot is located in a concrete block which is sunk about ten inches in the ground. To turn the valve, you have to stick your hand down that hole.

The other night, after having told my fourteen-year-old daughter to hurry up and get her shower, I went to bed. Jackie was already asleep when I heard this strange gurgling in the heating unit at the end of the hall. I suddenly remembered I had forgotten to reopen the valve after I washed the car that afternoon. That meant the water was either getting ready to overflow out of the heating units into the house, or it was flooding the back yard. I jumped out of bed, grabbed my flashlight, and raced down the stairs to the back door.

The back yard was flooded. Sloshing through the icy water in my bare feet, getting my pajamas wet up to my knees, I dashed to the pump house where I cut off all water to the house. Then I headed out across the pitch black yard, feeling my way between the pines and palmetto patches, to the edge of the pasture where the underground valve is located.

Kneeling in the cold mud beside the sunken valve, I foolishly forgot to look down the hole with my flashlight before putting my hand in there. When I put my hand in the hole I felt something move. Something slimy.

I withdrew my hand at great speed and, at the same time, leaped high off the ground from my kneeling position. Unfortunately, I had forgotten I was directly beneath the barbed wire fence. The result was disastrous.

When I became a Christian, I lost most of my old vocabulary. This robs me of the necessary safety valve to handle such emergencies. So, instead of cursing, I threw my flashlight. Unfortunately, it landed in the middle of the pond—leaving me in total darkness.

Ripping myself loose from the barbed wire, I staggered backwards away from the fence. In the process, I stepped in doggie-do. Hopping around in the high grass, I ran a thorny briar between my big toe and the toe right next door—in a place where nothing harsher than a washcloth had been in thirty years.

That which I lost I suddenly found—and a torrent of expletives issued forth, waking everyone in the house. Lights were flashing on all over the place as I went crashing through the shrubs, my pajamas ripped half-off, my back and neck bleeding, roaring back to the house in order to blame someone.

I had stopped to wash my foot off in the flooded back yard when I heard my daughter shouting from upstairs, "Hey, I'm all soaped up and there's no water in the shower."

Although I was back in control with the choice of words, I didn't seem to be able to control the volume. Thus I informed her, with a roar which could have been heard a mile away, that there was plenty of water down where I was and if she was unhappy she ought to join me.

Jackie finally came down the stairs in her bathrobe and we got the valve shut and the water turned back on. We never did find out what that slithery thing was in the hole.

For years I have been teaching that while the American church applauds accomplishment as the mark of success, God is more interested in what we become along the way than whether we arrive.

I am not sure what I became that night. But one thing is certain. I have not yet arrived.

THE LAST WORD

Not only am I out a brand new three-battery flashlight, but I ruined a perfectly good pair of pajamas and had to undergo three weeks of laughing, humiliating ridicule from my children who couldn't let me forget it was mom who had to come down and twist all the valves and then lead me back up the stairs to the safety of my bed.

Fortunately, no one else knows. You see, we live in the country where things are quiet.

2. And Now, the Announcements

For years churches have been plagued with something in the order of worship called *announcements*. Like vaccinations and haircuts, they are seen as necessities which at best can only be tolerated.

The importance of *announcements* can usually be graded by the person who is called upon to make them. Certainly no pastor, especially if he wears a robe, would make an *announcement* about the plugged drain in the men's room. Such *announcements* are best made by one of the lay leaders in the congregation under the guise of discipleship training.

Where to put the *announcements* was always a problem with me. As pastor of a large church several years ago, I determined they should always occupy the place right after the opening hymn and just before the pastoral prayer. Since people were still trying to get their kids quieted down, replace their hymn books in the racks, and put their purses on the floor, I figured we'd fill the void by making *announcements.*

I always worked on the theory that nobody ever listened anyway. One morning I deliberately *announced* that we would not have a water baptism service that night as planned since there was an alligator in the tank. The only alert person in that congregation of almost a thousand people was an eight-year-old boy who came up to me after the service and offered to catch the " 'gator" for me. He said if I'd get down in the tank and thrash around the " 'gator" would come out of his hiding place and then we could catch him with a special stick with a rope loop on one end.

Nobody else had ears to hear.

One pastor used to brag that he never made *announcements* in the worship service. "We're not here to make *announcements,*" he said with dignity. "We are here to worship the Lord."

It all sounded like a grand concept until I attended one of his services and heard his pastoral prayer. "O Lord, bless the women's meeting which will be held in the church social hall Tuesday at 7:00 P.M. And Lord, bless Miss Susie Short, that wonderful old retired missionary from Japan who has just returned from a trip around the world, as she speaks following the covered dish supper. . . ."

Now I am involved in a different kind of church that doesn't have a formal order of worship. This has presented a problem because we never know where to make the *announcements.* For a while we let everybody in the congregation stand up and make his own *announcements.* This was about as terrifying as trying to wade across a lake on thin ice. We never knew when somebody might announce a meeting of the Ku Klux Klan or some brother might use the time to stand up and preach a forty-five-minute sermon.

We decided we needed more decency and order in the service and *announced* that anyone with an *announcement* would have to come to the front and clear it with the presiding elder for his evaluation before sharing it with the congregation. That, at least, seemed scriptural. That is, if you can picture Ezekiel announcing a wedding shower for one of the Israelite maidens—followed by a time of refreshments.

While in the Philippines I heard of an *announcement* to end all *announcements.* In the far north of the island of Luzon a group of natives formed a church. Never exposed to civilization, they sent one of their elders into the city to find out how the "civilized" believers conducted their worship services. The elder returned saying, "We're doing everything wrong. We don't even have any *announcements.* All we do is meet and worship and praise and study the Bible and exhort one another to walk in the Spirit."

"Very well," the church decided, "then we must have *announcements.*" And forthwith they appointed one of the new native believers to be in charge of making the *announcements* the following Sunday.

Sunday rolled around and the natives all met to worship. There was much praise and singing and speaking from the Word. Then, with great solemnity, the pastor arose and said it was time for the *announcements.*

The new believer, who had been commissioned to make the *announcements,* rose to his feet and came to the pulpit. Clearing his throat, he said, "I wish to *announce* that Jesus Christ is Lord."

There was a great roar of applause and from that time on, so it is reported, the *announcements* have become the favorite part of the service. In fact, it is reported that sometimes as many as fifty persons stand to make their *announcement.*

Ah! Refreshing!

3. *It Was Written*

There is an ancient turquoise mine, high in the Sinaitic wilderness near Serabit el-Khadim, where the Egyptians mined precious stone more than a thousand years before the Exodus. Scratched on the walls of this darkened cave are characters which most archeological experts agree are the very beginnings of our modern day alphabet. In other words, the mines of Serabit el-Khadim are the birthplace of writing as we know it today—forty-five hundred years later.

Known as Proto-Sinaitic characters, the inscriptions mark the first time man was able to turn from the "picture letters" of the Egyptian hieroglyphics—an impossible system which contained more than three thousand characters—to form an alphabet of just a few letters. The people of the Sinai later taught this alphabet to the Phoenicians, who later taught it to the Greeks, who passed it along to us.

A small group of us on an archeological tour, tracing the

9

footsteps of Moses across the burning desert and incredibly high, craggy mountains of the Sinai, climbed the five-thousand-foot Serabit el-Khadim with our Jewish guide to enter the caves and view these inscriptions.

Even after all these centuries, the chisel marks were still evident where the mine supervisor, perhaps a nomadic friend of Abraham, had left his inscriptions in his newly-developed language.

Our guide, one of the top archeological authorities in Israel, told of having brought a small group of Harvard linguists to this same spot two years before. After having climbed the steep mountain, scaling walls and clambering over huge boulders, they came to the entrance of the mine. She said one of the linguists, an older man with white hair, stood before the inscriptions with tears running down his face. When she asked him what was wrong, he said, "I never dreamed I would one day stand at the birthplace of the alphabet."

One message contained practical instructions for the miners. "You shall give Abubu eight portions of. . . ." The last words were obliterated.

This is one of the major purposes of all writing—to pass along practical instructions as an extension of the mind and voice.

The other inscription contained the second purpose of writing—to convey spiritual truth. It was a three-word inscription which said simply, "God is eternal."

This time it was my turn to weep. For here, a thousand years before God thundered down His law to Moses from nearby Mount Sinai, He had already revealed himself in a still, small voice to a humble miner.

The turquoise of the Sinai is of poor quality. The Egyptians soon discovered that it faded and became worthless. They deserted the mines. But the message left behind in the turquoise mine is priceless—and will endure for all time. God is eternal!

4. *The Chambered Dreamer*

There is, living inside every one of us, a frustrated idealist. This quiet entity, who resides in the chest of every man and woman, is the one who whispers in the silence of the night, or cries out in those flushed moments following some willful sin, saying, "I will do better next time."

Our chambered dreamer is especially vocal during the early years of our life. In childhood he sees all things as possible. He tells us we have the capabilities of handling a big, red fire truck, or defending our home against a thousand pirates who are even now storming the beach, or even believing we might be elected president of the United States.

In adolescence he is the one who whispers in our ear, as we lie on our backs watching white clouds scudding through an azure blue sky, that all we need to make us happy is the love of a woman, or a man. He inspires us to write page after page of poetry, to begin the great American novel, or to pen some profound essay on God—all with ballpoint pen on lined paper torn from the back of a biology notebook. He satisfies us with dreams of making a million before we're thirty, of being named to the All-American team, of walking down the stage at Atlantic City as Miss America, of playing the lead role in a Hollywood extravaganza, or traveling to some far-off land as a dedicated missionary.

By the time we reach middle age, however, we have so buried this better self beneath heaps of failures, frustrations, and fat that the only time we hear from him is when we knowingly sin, or do less than we know we can do. At that time he still speaks, faintly, reminding us there is within us a person better than we are. We may not ever make it to the White House, or even become foreman of our shift, but by jiminey, we don't have to remain a failure, either. With God's help our dreams—or at least some portion of them—can come true.

As a boy I would occasionally follow my father's business partner, John W.E. Wheeler, around the golf course. Uncle John, as we affectionately called him, was never long off the tee. A diminutive man, he just didn't have the power to sock the ball very far. But he was always straight down the fairway—one hundred yards at a clip.

One afternoon, however, I was standing behind him on the number three tee when he connected just right. The driver hit the ball with a solid "click" and it was airborne, far past the two-hundred-yard marker, and rolled to a stop in perfect position for an eagle chip and putt. Mopping his bald head, Uncle John turned and said with his dry, Indiana wit: "Now remember that shot, Jamie boy. That's the true me."

Uncle John would probably never hit another shot as good as that. The next tee he was back to his old one hundred yards right down the middle. But he kept at it. For he knew, and now I knew also, that inside John Wheeler beat the spirit of a Bobby Jones, and, hopefully, one day, the "true him" would emerge once again.

That's the reason when we hear Patrick Henry talk about liberty or death, or Nathan Hale as he stands proudly on the gallows giving his one life for his country, our real self stands erect—for inside each of us beats the heart of a hero.

We see O.J. Simpson gallop through a mass of tangled arms and legs, or hear Beverly Sills strike a perfect note, or listen as Billy Graham says it just the way we like—and we say, "That's the way I'd do it, too, if I had the chance."

But most never have—or take—the chance. And so we content ourselves with lesser goals—equally unattainable:

"Beginning tomorrow I will lose forty pounds."

"This is my last cigarette."

"Starting in the morning I shall be the spiritual leader of my home."

All impossible goals. Yet each one is an extension of our real self—the expression of the yearnings and longings of whom we believe, in our heart of hearts, we really are.

Is it true: "All things are possible with God"? Yes. But only when we cooperate with the Father. John Masefield, the marvelous poet who gave us "I must go down to the seas again, to the lonely sea and the sky," also gave us a lesser known poem, the cry of his own soul.

Oh yesterday our little troop was ridden through and
    through,
Our swaying, tattered pennons fled, a broken, beaten few,
And all a summer afternoon they hunted us and slew;
But tomorrow,
By the living God, we'll try the game again!

Only those who dare to dream of victory, will ever succeed.

while he was mowing his grass, his little three-year-old girl knocked over a jar of gasoline in the utility room. There was an explosion and most of her skin was burned off. Roy beat out the flames with his hands and then sat with her for a week in the hospital as her life slipped away. Just an hour before she died I rode the elevator with him in the hospital. His burned hands were bandaged and I had to push the button for him. But as he stepped off the elevator outside her room, he was whistling. What did Roy have to whistle about?

B.C. Bledsoe had bone cancer. The doctors sent him home from the hospital to die. He was in horrible pain. The minute you walked into the house you could smell the odor of death. "Go on back into the bedroom," his wife told me. "He'd like to see you." As I walked down the hall I could hear, coming from B.C.'s room, a cracked, off-key sound. I softly opened the door. Lying on his bed, tears of pain running down his cheeks, the old man was singing. What did B.C. have to sing about?

A.D. Croft was a blind preacher in the hills of South Carolina. He pastored four rural churches. His wife drove him everywhere he went. The last time I was with him he gave out with a big belly laugh, hugged my neck, and roared, "I'll be seeing you." What does a blind man have to laugh about?

A Protestant chaplain told of walking through a rice paddy with a South Vietnamese Catholic soldier. Suddenly the soldier stepped on a land mine. It blew off both legs at the hips. The chaplain said he cradled the young man's head in his lap while the lifeblood pumped out of his body into the muddy water. It was just a matter of seconds before he would be gone. There was no way to communicate since neither spoke the other's language. Then the chaplain remembered a phrase from an ancient Latin liturgy. Looking down into the ashen face of the dying soldier, he said, *"Sursum corda"* ("Lift up your heart"). There was a surprised look of recognition. Then with a final smile, the soldier gave the congregation's response, *"Regem habemas"* ("We lift them up unto the Lord").

That's the one thing that Charlotte Adkins, Joe Snyder, Roy Mathis, B.C. Bledsoe, A.D. Croft and the dying soldier had in common. They all had a Lord to whom they could lift up their hearts.

When the blackness of pain and grief wraps itself around our lives. When it seems all hope has gone and nothing remains but despair. Then we can lift up our hearts. Before us is an open tomb. We have a King.

He lives.

His name is Jesus.

6. The Old Man in My Future

Someday, down the road, you're going to meet an old man. Out there—ten, twenty, thirty years—he'll be waiting for you. You'll be catching up with him, for he'll be you.

What kind of old man will he be? Will he be a seasoned, gentle, gracious man, surrounded by those who love and respect him? Or will he be a bitter, grouchy, cynical old buzzard without a good word for anyone? Sour and alone?

The kind of man you'll be depends on what you are now. In my teenage son's room hangs a motto for him to see every day. It says simply: "You're fast becoming what you're going to be."

My son, me, you . . . we're going to be the composite of everything we see, hear, say, think, do, and wish today—tomorrow. Our minds are being set in molds, strapped in place by today's attitudes. We'll turn out only what we put in.

Someplace out of my past I recall a story of a preacher who took his son with him to a small country church where he was the guest minister. At the door was an offering box, into which, after thought, he dropped a quarter. At the end of the day the treasurer presented the cleric with the box, explaining it contained the love offering from the church. Opening the box, the minister saw, in the dust of the bottom, his one quarter. His little son said it well: "Daddy, if you'd put more in, you'd get more out."

And so it is with those of us growing older.

When I was considering marriage as a young man, a wise friend counseled me, saying, "If you want to know what kind of woman you're going to have thirty years from now, look at her mother."

I did. I liked what I saw and went ahead with the marriage. Time has proved my friend right, much to my pleasure. To a real extent my wife has become what her mother put into her as a child.

Last year I met a man who called himself The Great Salvador. From sleight-of-hand artist and card shark in old vaudeville, he later consorted with some of the world's great entertainers. Yet his life was made up of a long series of "almosts" because he refused to submit to discipline. Today he is a pickpocket in Atlanta. He has become what he was.

The only thing that can break this chain of inherited and environmental fatalism is an intrusion of God into the life of a person. God, and God alone, can keep me from becoming the sum total of my past. Even though I still carry the seeds and scars of yesteryear, it's possible for me to become what St. Paul calls a "new creature." Thus, my ancestry changes and I literally become a child of a King.

Now after years of trying to pull myself up by my bootstraps and failing, I gladly consent to let God take what's left—to remake me in His own image. Meanwhile, I excitedly look forward to meeting that old man in my future.

7. Rejected

It was eighty miles from Nazareth to Bethlehem. The rocky trail wound south to the border of Samaria, across the Jordan River (no good Jew would defile himself by traveling through Samaria), down the east side of the Jordan through what was known as "the wilderness," then back up those final miles on the Jericho Road. It was a tortuous trip, and the last miles were the hardest—almost straight up the side of the mountains. It took almost a week to make the agonizing trip by foot and donkey.

But it was agonizing in more ways than one for Joseph and Mary. Both were probably teenagers, Mary perhaps sixteen at the time—and pregnant, well into her ninth month and expecting her baby any day. Riding the hard back of that donkey, being jarred with every step, must have caused excruciating pain.

Besides this, they were traveling alone. Yes, there were others traveling from Nazareth to Bethlehem to be counted in the census ordered by the Roman emperor, Augustus. But the townspeople back in Nazareth shunned them—ostracized them. You see, Mary was a social outcast. Although engaged, she admitted she was pregnant out of wedlock. What possible explanation could she have made that would have sounded believable? Who would believe a wild story about a visitation from an angel saying, "Hail, Mary, full of grace"? And a virgin conception?

Only with her cousin Elizabeth, an old woman who was herself pregnant, could Mary share her concern. Even Joseph would have deserted her had it not been for a special visit from an angel.

Now the question pounded in her temples with every jolting step of the donkey: "How can I ever return to Nazareth with my baby? Will they treat Him as they have treated me?" Little did she know it would be three years before she would be able to return home.

And then those final terrifying miles up the Jericho Road, dark, winding, rocky, narrow, with thieves lurking in the caves.

It was cold that night in Bethlehem when they arrived. "No room, Nazarene. Can't you see that my inn is already full of important guests? You and your wench will have to sleep in the stable tonight."

What thoughts must have accompanied them as they made their way behind the inn into the dank cave where the animals slept. Alone. Friendless. Hungry. Cold. Shut out.

And Joseph. What faith. How he must have loved this dainty child with her stomach protruding under her dress. He had nothing more than the word of an angel that God was in it all.

They prepared for the night of pain and fright in the filthy, foul-smelling, cold stable. No doctor. No hospital. Not even a midwife. Before dawn, Mary would scream in pain, and Joseph, awkwardly, would receive the baby from her body.

Rejected

Born alone in the filth and dung of a stable. Born to be despised and rejected of men. Born to be misunderstood. Born to be lonely. Born to be hated. Born to be tortured and killed between two "common" thieves.

And yet out of that night, that horrible holy night, arising out of His fellowship with the common, the soiled, the filthy, the impure . . . came the Savior of the world. God's own Son—at whose name every knee would eventually bow. Bow, innkeeper! Bow, important guests! Bow, gossipy old women back in Nazareth! Bow, Herod. Bow, Roman soldiers. Bow, Augustus Caesar. The King is here. King Jesus!

> For unto you is born this day in the city of David a Savior, which is Christ the Lord. (Luke 2:11)

So take heart, all ye whom the world calls common. Take heart all you misunderstood youth, all you heartbroken parents, all you cast out children, all you drug addicts, all you alcoholics, all you prisoners, all you unwed mothers, all you lonely, sad and left-out ones. God uses the forsaken, the rejected, the despised, the lonely, the unlovely, the ugly.

God knows what it's like to be that way. For He was like that, too, on that Silent Night in Bethlehem.

8. Wanderers and Pilgrims

The speaker at church last Sunday, De Vern Fromke, pointed out the difference between a pilgrim and a wanderer.

He was referring to those Israelites in the book of Exodus who left Egypt as pilgrims—but became wanderers, spending forty years in the wilderness of Sinai.

According to Fromke, a pilgrim may do a lot of wandering, but he has direction. He knows where he is going. A wanderer, on the other hand, has no goal. He has lost his direction. Both are on the move, but only one is going anywhere.

I thought back to Harry Gasque. Old Harry was a wanderer. Back when I was pastor of a Baptist church in South Carolina, I had my office on busy U.S. 25. About twice a year Old Harry would ramble into my study on his way north or south—depending on the season. He was a hobo, in his mid-sixties, with wrinkled face, watery eyes and a toothless grin.

I enjoyed seeing him for he represented a life style which

inwardly I envied. Unlike me, locked in my plush office with carpet on the floors and books of theology on the shelves, Harry was a free spirit. He was not controlled by a calendar or a committee.

One spring morning Old Harry stopped by to chat. He was headed north, he said, to Asheville, North Carolina. He tried on several pair of mismatched shoes from our "care closet," turned down my invitation to lunch ("I don't want to feel obligated," he grinned), and was on his way. Everything he owned was in his battered old cardboard suitcase.

Shortly afterwards I left the office and spotted Harry along the highway—hitchhiking south.

"I thought you were going north," I said as I waited for the traffic light to change.

"Well," he said, spitting a stream of tobacco juice on the sidewalk, "it seems most of the traffic is headed south. So, I just crossed the road and decided to head on down to Augusta instead."

Harry Gasque, with all his freedom, was a wanderer. He had no goal.

Actually, I guess he's not much different from the busy charismatic executive who bounced off the airplane in a large city, jumped in a cab and said to the driver, "Take me anyplace. I've got business everywhere."

Sheep aren't the only ones who wander. So do shepherds. They don't do much damage as long as they move slowly—and have a small flock. But let an insecure man get in a hurry and he becomes a destroyer—running over structures, bashing down time-tested principles, ripping up roots trying to find himself and prove to the world that he's a success.

Pilgrims aren't like this. They may have a carefree attitude, but they also have purpose. They know where they are going.

The true filling of the Spirit brings stability. Not the kind that keeps us from moving, but the kind that gives direction to our movement. Otherwise we wander from ministry to ministry, job to job, church to church, doctrine to doctrine—always looking, never finding.

Ten years ago when I moved into the charismatic dimension I entered as a free-floater—a helium filled balloon. I was every place the wind of the Spirit was blowing. Conferences. Prayer groups. Conventions. I felt I had been called to meet every need. I hardly had time for my family, much less to obey God.

Now I realize that unless freedom has restraints, it leads to wandering. The free-floater may give the impression of liberty, but actually he's no different than Old Harry who was scared to death of strings.

The hardest kind of discipline—and the most necessary—is the discipline of submitting to one another. God not only looses those bound with chains, but he sets the solitary in families (Psalm 68:6). And living together is the hardest discipline of all.

In the midst of his soaring passage in Ephesians 4-5, where he encourages us to fulfill our God-given ministries, Paul warns us to temper our call with submission.

The man who says, "I submit only to God" is just as foolish as the man who says, "I submit only to my shepherd." Our spiritual family consists not just of me and the Trinity, nor of me and those in covenant relationship with me—it is made up of "other sheep which are not of this fold," also.

Free-wheeling charismatics need to have their strings attached to keep them from doing crazy things. Those in the "discipleship movement" need to learn to soar again.

The cry is for balance.

Recently a man wandered through our community on his way to nowhere. He justified his wandering by quoting 1 Corinthians 7:23. "Ye are bought with a price, be not ye the servants of men."

He was angered, and soon moved on, when I suggested he needed to read on to 1 Corinthians 9:19 where Paul added, "For though I be free from all men, yet have I made myself servant unto all, that I might gain the more."

God has a clear word for the church today: Quit ostracizing your brothers. Submit to one another. Enter corporate life. Come into order for the perfecting of the saints.

It is the only way we'll ever cease our wandering—and enter Canaan.

9. Alone

I parked my car, shut off the headlights, and walked back to the little knot of people who were standing beside the darkened highway.

Lying on his back with body grotesquely bent was a man. He had been struck by a car. Both shoes had been knocked off by the impact which had picked up his body and smashed it against the windshield. Little bits of flesh and hair were still imbedded in the shattered glass and twisted windshield wiper.

The crowd seemed strangely disinterested in the man's body. Someone had thrown a dirty canvas tarp over his legs as though this were as close as he wished to get. Little groups of people stood around talking to each other. Two of the men had cans of beer in their hands, having just stepped outside of a roadside joint nearby.

I knelt beside the man and heard him breathing. The neon lights from the tavern cast weird reflections on his twisted body. His eyes were open and glassy. His breath sounded like someone sucking on a straw in a nearly empty milkshake cup.

THE LAST WORD

I put my hand on his chest but quickly removed it. It felt like a plastic bag filled with water. I turned his head so the blood would run out of his mouth rather than back down his throat. I tried to brush some of the dirt and gravel from his face, but it all seemed so futile. I looked up from my kneeling position but the people were still standing in little groups several feet away. No one offered to help.

He stopped breathing for long agonizing seconds, then came another gurgling gasp. His body was straining to stay alive, although I had the impression his spirit had already departed.

I bent low over him to try to speak, but the smell of cheap liquor was so strong it forced me back. He was dying—maybe dead—drunk.

The ambulance arrived and the attendants gently placed his dirty, torn body on a stretcher and sped off into the night. I knew the report would read DOA—dead on arrival.

After talking to the patrolman who had arrived, I walked back to my car. I caught snatches of conversation—"been in every bar along the road" .   "staggered into the path of a speeding car on the fourlane."

A fat man, silhouetted in the door of the honky-tonk, muttered to a friend, "Serves him right. He deserved to get hit after acting the way he did in here."

I wondered if he would feel the same way if it had been his son—and shuddered involuntarily as I realized he probably would.

The paper the next morning said the man was estranged from his wife and four children. Had no friends. Had been fired from his job. Belonged to no church.

That was a number of years ago. But I remember it took me several days to scrub the bloodstains from my hands. However, I finally got them clean, in time for church services Sunday where we sat in our cozy building and sang songs about how much we loved one another.

10. Homesick

It was Tuesday morning and a small group had gathered at the nursing home behind the hospital for a weekly Bible study. At the close of the period, the leader asked, "Does anybody have a need we can pray about?"

I looked at the wrinkled faces in the room. Does anyone have a need? All they had were needs. Three were in wheelchairs. The rest were sitting in a rough semi-circle on those flimsy porch chairs with the plastic webbing. Some were staring straight ahead. All had the look of the forgotten on their faces.

One of the wheelchair ladies, a silver-haired woman with only the stump of one leg sticking out from under her soiled gown, shyly lifted her hand.

"Please, would you pray for me? It's Thanksgiving time, and I miss my daddy."

The old man sitting next to her stirred from his semi-slumber. "How long has he been gone?"

THE LAST WORD

"He died in 1914," she answered. Her eyes filled with tears and her chin began to quiver. "At Thanksgiving daddy would walk around the big table and lay his hands on our heads, asking God to bless us." She began to sob. "I'm so homesick."

I looked around the room. It was the Tuesday before Thanksgiving. All the heads were nodding. They wanted to go home, too—but they didn't know where it was.

Who said homesickness was limited to kids who go to summer camp or young folks away at school? Homesickness is built into every one of us. It is that inner longing that draws us back to the time when we felt most loved, most protected, most secure.

Who among us, from runaway child wandering the lonely streets of a strange city, to the forgotten aged in some nursing home, has not wished for loving arms to rock him to sleep? For a mother's breast to lean upon? For a father's arm around a shoulder when things are tough? Who among us has not, in times of deep fear, wanted to curl back into a fetal position and cry, "Somebody be a daddy to me—just for tonight"?

The one person in history who had the greatest right to be homesick was Jesus. Look at what He left behind. Yet He only talked of what lay ahead.

I caught a glimpse of that on Tuesday morning before Thanksgiving. Earthly daddies and mothers die. The old homesites, once so precious, fall into decay or are destroyed. Only the faded memories linger to haunt our loneliness. Homesickness is the backward call into a world to which we can never return. Faith is lifting up our feeble eyes and fixing them on another Father who stands in the future, beckoning us onward.

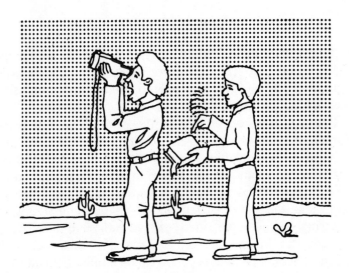

11. How Do You Handle a Tidal Wave?

Ever since I was awakened by an early morning earth tremor last year, I've spent a lot of time thinking about last things. Most Floridians had never experienced an earthquake. However, I had just returned from New Guinea where I had gone through a real live, teeth-jarring, road-buckling, mountain-toppling "guria." To be at home in what I thought was the safest place in the world, my Florida bed, and suddenly feel the same sensations caused me no little mind-searching.

Now aside from the fact that a host of prophecies were confirmed that night (and a lot more came into being), our family did learn some things from that mini-quake which rocked our house for a few seconds. It forced us to think about the importance of material things. I mean, if you have thirty seconds to get out of your house before it is swallowed up in a yawning chasm, it seems well to plan ahead what you'd try to salvage.

In an after-dinner conference the next evening, I allowed

each child the privilege of deciding on two things to take with them in case they had to leap for safety in the middle of the night. (My wife had already declared, pragmatically, that she'd take her houserobe and glasses.)

The children opted for things like their Bibles, an almost-completed school research paper, or the cat (Mrs. Robinson). I stated this was a waste of time because it is impossible to catch Mrs. Robinson in thirty seconds.

Our daughter Sandy said she would not leave unless she could take the twenty-seven stuffed animals she sleeps with every night. When I reminded her she was limited to two things, she said she'd take her mom and me. That was such a nice thought, even if we were second to the stuffed animals, that I declared I'd clear the table. The children headed for the TV room while mom took the flashlight and went out to inspect the yard—just in case a yawning chasm might be appearing in the flower bed.

We had just finished reading several prophecies predicting that Florida would break off and slide into the sea. One "prophet," after mailing out his prophecies, announced it just so happened he had a farm in the Carolinas. For a very reasonable price, Floridians could purchase a lot on his farm and so escape the coming disaster.

(He reminded me of my high school football coach who insisted every boy should wear a certain kind of football shoe. The shoe could be purchased only at the coach's sporting goods store.)

All this raises the question of the multitude of last day prophecies sweeping the world. Several years ago the nation was swamped with rumors of hitchhikers who got in people's cars, said that Jesus was coming soon, and then disappeared. These ranged from bearded hippies to little old women in tennis shoes. The only trouble was, I never was able to talk to anyone who actually picked up one of these characters. It was always "a friend told me he had heard."

Shortly afterwards there was a bevy of photographs that appeared. They were of a gowned and bearded figure surrounded by clouds. One woman told me the photo was taken by her aunt in Miami. Another was taken by a woman who spied the figure in the Nebraska clouds and leaped from her car just in time to snap the picture before "he" disappeared. Still another said the figure appeared over an Hawaiian volcano. All were the same photograph.

When I asked the people what the figure was to represent, they all said it was a warning that Christ was coming soon. I'm afraid I disappointed them with my lack of enthusiasm. The Bible gives us far more warning than signs in the sky. And even if I weren't skeptical of darkroom techniques, it bothers me that so many of us are gullible, looking for signs to titillate our emotions rather than trusting in the Word of God.

Next came the earthquake prophecies, starting with California and moving to Florida. These were followed by a rash of prophecies centering around the comet Kohoutek—which God just seemed to brush out of the sky. Later there were tidal wave prophecies.

Jesus said in the last days we would have false prophets, many performing great signs and wonders, saying of the coming Lord: "Behold, he is in the desert. Behold, he is in the secret chambers." Believe it not, Jesus said. When he comes we won't need a photograph to prove it.

Any prophecy which takes our eyes off the Living Christ and causes us to focus on cloud images, bearded hippies, old women in tennis shoes, or causes us to move to the mountains or jungle to "prepare" for the tribulation, is not of God. Even if we Christians go through the tribulation, it shall not be in fear, for the promises of God are just as valid in the tribulation as they are in the millennium.

How, then, should Christians react when faced with false

prophecy? First, don't try to convince through argument. I remember a sign on a public bus in Bangkok which said simply, "Do not argue with the driver when he is drunk."

Instead, realize the purpose of such nonsense is to "deceive the very elect." Christians have nothing to fear—not earthquake, fire, flood, famine, or tribulation. Remember, nothing can separate us from the love of Christ.

Last year a frantic woman called our house in the middle of the night. She said she'd just received a call saying a giant tidal wave was about to engulf the state of Florida. What should she do?

I said, "Shout, 'Hallelujah!' If it is true, we'll all see Jesus before dawn. If it is not true, another false prophet has been revealed. Either way—we win."

12. Upstaged

Everyone knows that having one's name appear in headlines on the sports page is one of the most fleeting of all claims to fame. Who cares today, for instance, that on a soggy November night in 1953 I kicked an extra point to win a football game for good old Vero Beach High School? Yet, to me, seeing my name in the subhead of the following week's *Press Journal*—"Buckingham kicks PAT"—seemed to sort of enshrine me in the halls of football immortality. Surely, I thought, everyone in town would clip that section of the paper and read it over and over for years to come—carrying it around something like they did with Wilt Chamberlain's size sixteen shoes on the Freedom Train. But no one cared—or cares. In fact, even my own copy of the paper has yellowed and crumbled, and when I try to tell my children about my football prowess, they yawn—or even worse, giggle. Ah, fame, what a fickle lover you are.

But I've discovered something even more fleeting than having your name in the headlines of tomorrow's fish wrapper. It's having your name flash in lights on the scoreboard of Dodger Stadium in Los Angeles, when out of 26,982 paying customers, only your wife and children know who you are.

Even so, it was quite a thrill.

Recently I was in Los Angeles to autograph books at a booksellers convention. Chuck Benedict, an old friend and one of the top sportscasters on the West Coast, got our entire family VIP tickets for the afternoon game between the Dodgers and Cardinals. What I didn't know was that Chuck, who worked in the public relations department of the L.A. Rams, also had contacts with the man who was responsible for flashing those electronic messages on the huge board next to the scoreboard.

Chuck kept the whole thing secret, but throughout the game kept asking me if my camera was ready for any unexpected action. Then, during the last half of the sixth inning, with the Dodgers leading 6-2, and with first baseman Steve Garvey at the plate, the children began to squeal and point at the electronic board over the left field bleachers.

The lights were flashing. "Dodger Stadium proudly welcomes Jamie Buckingham and his wife Jackie. . . ."

I grabbed my camera. Something inside told me if I didn't capture it on film, it would be like Bobby Burns' snow falling in the river—"a moment white then gone forever." I could hear the crowd applauding as I snapped away. But it wasn't me they recognized. In fact, no one had seen the sign. All eyes were on Steve Garvey as he raced around first base with a double to center field. My last chance for fame in the sports arena, and I had been upstaged.

Then to top it all off, I discovered I had forgotten to remove the lens cap. I returned to my seat, discouraged, only to find it isn't in the applause of the crowd that one finds security, it's in the love of his family. The kids gathered around, laughing and clapping me on the back. "Good old pop, he finally made it."

I looked back at Chuck and grinned. He knew. What's a yellowed newspaper when compared with the love of children? As long as I'm a success in their eyes, nothing else matters.

13. Honesty Costs

The little old lady at the counter of the 14th Avenue store must have been approaching eighty. I was standing behind her and couldn't help but overhear the conversation.

The day before she had purchased a small book for twenty-five cents and now had come back to buy another for a friend. As the clerk wrapped the package, the lady noticed the price was thirty-five cents. "But I only paid a quarter yesterday," she said. The clerk was kind but firm. "No ma'am, the price has been the same all week."

The old woman dug into her ancient handbag and came out with the correct change. "I'm sorry I was such a bother," she smiled at the clerk and turned to leave.

I stepped forward to pay for my purchase when suddenly the old lady reappeared. She looked at me and apologized saying, "I'm sorry to interrupt you, but there is one more thing I must discuss with this young lady." I was in no hurry so I stepped back and waited.

The old woman laid her handbag on the counter, unsnapped the top, and began to rummage around inside. Looking up she smiled apologetically and said, "I hate to be such a bother." The clerk looked at the long line that was beginning to form behind the cash register and said graciously, "That's all right, ma'am, take your time."

The old woman laid her pocketbook on the counter and then removed her shawl and laid it on a chair. Very gingerly she began to remove the items from her purse. I was beginning to take an intense interest in what was going on.

The crowd around the cash register had grown larger and the clerk looked up—helplessly. Finally the old lady reached the bottom of her purse and came up with a single dime. Turning to the clerk she said, "I forgot I only paid you twenty-five cents for the booklet yesterday—when I should have paid thirty-five cents. I owe you another dime."

"Oh, no, that's all right," the young clerk said, trying to refuse the dime. The old lady was insistent. "It's the only honest thing to do."

A gruff-looking man with a dead cigar in his mouth who had been waiting with the rest of us spoke up with surprising tenderness. "You're right, little mother. It always pays to be honest."

"Oh, no," the little lady answered, looking up at him as she stuffed the items back into her old purse. "It costs to be honest. It just cost me a dime." Then she added, "But Jesus is honest and I try to be like Him."

She turned and hobbled out. The whole store seemed to brighten up a bit. And unless I am mistaken, there was just a glint of a tear in the eye of the clerk as she pushed the key on the cash register and rang up—ten cents.

14. Real Men

We men, we're pretty tough customers. We don't cry. We don't get scared. We have answers to every question our wives ask—and answers to some they don't ask. And we're very cautious about getting too emotional—especially when it comes to love. That kind of stuff is okay for women. In fact, we like 'em that way. But us guys are pretty tough.

At least that's the way I was raised. As a boy I never, never kissed my brothers. Or my daddy. We shook hands. That was the manly thing to do. My football coaches taught me to hit, and hit hard. If I whimpered when I got hit, I ran laps. My military instructor kicked the guys who cried, and ridiculed the ones who showed mercy. My supervisor on my first full-time job after college taught me to "stick it to 'em before they stick it to you."

I was all macho.

But several years ago my twisted thinking began to get straightened out. I received a letter from a young attorney in

North Carolina one day, scrawled in longhand on a yellow legal sheet. He was sharing the joys and challenges of his new walk with Jesus Christ, plus some deep, personal things. He closed the letter with "Love, Nard."

I was half-embarrassed and half-amused. "Why, that's the way a ten-year-old boy would sign a letter—'love,'" I thought. Then it occurred to me that Jesus had remarked, a long time ago, that only ten-year-old boys, and folks like them, could enter the Kingdom of Heaven. Stuffed shirts and macho men would just not feel comfortable in the midst of all that love and praise.

I had forgotten. In my haste to become a man, a really tough man, I had left out some of the most important ingredients which make up true manhood—including love. Somehow I had picked up the false impression that real men don't cry, or say "I love you" to other men.

I began to think about the way I signed my letters. Most of them were signed "Sincerely." Or, if I wanted to show some kind of affection, I would sign them "Yours truly." When I wanted to appear especially pious, I wrote "In the Master's service." To those closest to me I signed "In Christ's love."

Anything to keep from sounding childlike.

Anything to keep from saying "I love you."

Hollywood script writers have cheapened love until many Christian men are embarrassed to say "I love you." Legal religionists, on the other hand, have made us so fearful of the flesh that the sight of two men embracing threatens an entire church. J.B. Phillips, the conservative English scholar and translator, felt so strongly about this that he even rewrote the Bible. When he translated 1 Peter 5:14, where Peter literally says, "Salute one another with a kiss of love," the Phillips translation reads, "Give each other a handshake."

Recently it occurred to me that I had never, at least in my memory, kissed the man who means more to me than any man on earth—my father. I would visit him in his home in Vero Beach and find him sitting in his wheelchair, working on his books or writing at his desk. And we would shake hands. So one afternoon I made a special trip from Melbourne to Vero Beach—about forty miles—just to walk into the house and bend over, put my arms around my father, and kiss his cheek. It felt odd. Strange. But it made me cry. And he wept also.

I need to be loved. There is something in me that responds only to an embrace. It is not enough for someone to give me a cold-fish handshake and say, "I love the Jesus in you," or, "The Christ in me loves the Christ in you." I need someone to love the sinner in me. I need to be loved by someone else the way Jesus loves me—just as I am. I need to be around people who are not ashamed to embrace me, to greet me with a kiss, or to sign their letters "Love."

Last week I picked up the phone and called a retired businessman who occasionally writes a column in his church newsletter. Although I had never met him, I appreciated his writing. "I just want to tell you I love you," I said.

There was a long period of silence. Then with great emotion he said, "That's the first time a grown man has ever said those words to me, but God knows how I've longed to hear them."

A lot of things about me are changing. One of them is the way I sign my letters.

15. Why?

In the Amazon jungle of Peru, several years ago, I met an old Indian evangelist. He was no Billy Graham or Rex Humbard. He had never worn a suit and tie. In fact, he had never worn a pair of shoes. He had never been inside a church building or even heard the sound of a piano or pipe organ. But for more than twenty years, since he had become a Christian, he had lived among his primitive people, going from village to village telling the Indians about a God who cares. In a society where suicide is considered the only way out of the hopelessness, he had brought hope—for this life and the hereafter. He was known throughout the jungle as a "man of God."

Now he was horribly sick. His body was bent and twisted with the excruciating pain of arthritis. His hands were gnarled and misshapen. His feet bent backward at the ankles so even when he was able to drag himself erect, he had to stand on the sides of his insteps. On top of that, he had contracted jungle tuberculosis. All he could do was sit in front of his jungle hut and wait to die.

I visited him briefly that morning, squatting in the dirt in front of his thatched home. Despite the dirt and poverty, there was an aura of the Holy Spirit all around him as we talked.

"Many of my Indian friends ask me 'why?' " he said. "They say, 'You have served God all these years. You have renounced the false cures of the witch doctor. You have walked many miles through the jungle preaching the Gospel. You have laid hands on the sick and they have been healed. Now this. Why?' "

The bent little man smiled at me through his pain, exposing his rotting teeth and swollen gums. He brushed a fly from his wrinkled face. "I tell them if I would go into my hut and see Jesus sitting on the floor in the corner near the fire, I would not start asking Him 'Why?' No, I would put my face in the dirt and say, 'Jesus, I love you.' I no longer ask why. I just tell Jesus I love Him, and when I say that, nothing else matters."

I learned more from that bronzed old Indian with a tattered loincloth and twisted limbs, than I have learned from most of my learned professors. I learned there are some things in this world which cannot be reasoned out by logic, things which do not fit the mold of our Western, scientific minds. In many cases the answer to the question "why?" is purposefully withheld by a loving God. In other cases, the question "why?" is simply not the right question to ask. Satisfaction comes only when we worship, as the old Indian said, not when we continue to pound at the door of knowledge with our many questions, demanding answers.

I had forgotten about the old Indian until the early morning of the day I was to leave on a two-week camping/ hiking trip to the Sinai—a sort of religious pilgrimage under the guise of collecting research for another book. For weeks I had been thinking that as I returned to the Sinai and stood on the exact spot where Moses stood when he heard God's audible voice, I would be free to ask—and receive—answers to some of the deep questions of my life.

That morning, however, packing my things to catch the plane for New York and then on to Israel, I realized I had been planning amiss. Instead of asking—I was to worship.

And leave the answers to God.

16. *Don't Confuse Me with the Facts*

Eskimo stories, like Aesop's fables, seem to live forever. One of those which has been around a long time is credited to Carl Loman, the reindeer king of Alaska, who once told the story of a certain Greenland Eskimo. The Eskimo was brought to New York City for a short visit. When he returned to his native village near the North Pole, he told stories of buildings that rose into the clouds, of streetcars which he described as houses that moved along the trail with people living in them, of huge bridges, lights that have no fire and burn at night, and other dazzling miracles of civilization.

His people looked at him coldly and walked away. They changed his name to Sagdluk (The Liar). He carried the name in shame to his grave.

Years later, Knud Rasmussen traveled from Greenland to Alaska. He was accompanied by an Eskimo named Mitek (Eider Duck). Mitek visited Copenhagan and New York. Upon his return to Greenland he remembered the tragedy of Sagdluk. He decided it would not be wise to tell the truth. Instead, he would narrate stories that his people could grasp and save his reputation.

He told them how he and Dr. Rasmussen stayed in a camp on the banks of the great Hudson River. Each morning they would paddle their kayak out and hunt duck, geese, and seal. Mitek, in the eyes of his countrymen, was a very honest man. Even though he knew the truth, he was thoughtful enough not to offend his friends by speaking it. Therefore his neighbors treated him with rare respect.

The road of the teller of new truths has always been rocky. Socrates was forced to drink hemlock. Isaiah was fastened between two planks and "sawn asunder." Stephen was stoned. John Huss was burned at the stake. Galileo was terrified into retraction of his solar verities. Jesus was crucified, as were many of His followers. The bloody trail runs throughout the pages of history and is caught up in Jesus' almost pathetic words, "Oh, Jerusalem, Jerusalem, which killest the prophets, and stonest them that are sent unto thee. . . ." (Luke 13:34).

Most of us resent the impact of new ideas and look with suspicion on whomever imparts them to us. We hate to be disturbed in the beliefs and prejudices that have been handed down with the family furniture and church tradition. Concepts, even though found in the Bible, that God works through men to heal miraculously, that the gifts of the Spirit (including tongues) are for the church today, that most church government is of man rather than God—are all rejected. When such new ideas invade our congregations we rise up snarling from our winter sleep to chase them away.

The Eskimos may have had some excuse. Their simple minds were unable to visualize the pictures drawn by Sagdluk. But there is no adequate reason why modern man, especially one "made new in Jesus Christ," should ever close his mind to a fresh new "slant" on life.

The old Baptist deacon used to pray, "Lord, make me right the first time, because you know I never change my mind." And when the Methodist preacher prayed, "Lord, light a spark of revival in this dead church," one of his laymen chimed in with, "Amen, Lord, and we'll water that spark." Too true, too true!

Recently there was a great outpouring of the Holy Spirit on a mission compound deep in the heart of the Amazon jungle. Some of the old fundamentalists were set free to praise God in a new way. Others resisted. Then at a Wednesday night believers' meeting, one of the mission leaders rose to his feet.

"The Bible speaks of a great latter rain which shall fall on the people prior to the coming of the Lord Jesus," he said. "This rain is now falling all over the world, and here in the jungle as well. Some of you conservatives have raised your theological umbrellas, trying to ward off the torrent. But the power of God's Spirit is going to demolish even your umbrellas. If you're not careful, you'll find yourselves standing out in the rain, poking your stick at God."

Today's "charismatic" revelations are not "new" truths—they are simply a reenactment of truths which were evident in the first century church. Those hamstrung by prejudice and tradition will continue to stone the prophets. Too lazy to stretch their minds, they will forever water down the truth to keep from offending and thus remain satisfied with visions of kayaks on the Hudson River.

Others, perhaps, will go see for themselves and discover the houses that move along the trail and lights that have no fire.

17. *Walking in the Light*

Walking in the light is risky living. It calls for honesty, which is not only foreign to our nature, but threatens us as well. Yet in the process of becoming New Testament people (that's necessary, you know, before we can have a New Testament church), we have to shed our masks and run the risk of letting our brothers and sisters see us as we really are.

The risk involved is one of rejection. Many in the kingdom are unable, not only to be honest themselves, but to accept others who are honest. How much better, though, to be rejected by some in order to be accepted by those who really count—including the wonderful feeling of accepting ourselves.

This kind of transparency is not only the key to spiritual effectiveness, but to mental health, physical wholeness, and happy homes.

Whatever I would ordinarily say behind a brother's back, I must be willing to say to his face. Ordinarily we wait until our guests leave. Then I say to my wife, "Tom's really got some spiritual problems, doesn't he?" Or, "Did you notice the way Betty slapped her children?" Walking in the light, though, demands confrontation.

Last week Jackie and I had one of our infrequent arguments. (By that, I mean things are better than they used to be.) She had gone with me to Miami and we returned after dark. Early the next morning our son, Tim, woke me and confessed he had gotten the car stuck in a mudhole the afternoon before. The floorboards were filled with muddy slime. I sent him on to school and went to work trying to clean up the mess.

When Jackie came down an hour later to give me advice, I blew up. After I calmed down, I realized I had to do more than apologize. I had to walk in the light. That meant confession.

"I was angry because I blamed you," I said. "I felt had you stayed home yesterday this wouldn't have happened. When you slept late I was even angrier. I had more important things to do—spiritual things—than clean out the car. In short, I felt you were selfish and lazy."

She reacted in tears. "Now I know how you really feel about me!"

"Not feel. *Felt.* I was wrong. My feelings changed when I asked you to forgive me. However, you need to know how I felt so you can help me when I am wrong again in the future."

It was painful for both of us. Risky living always is. But the air is now clear. And because we are walking in the light, we have *fellowship* one with another.

18. Free at Last

She should have entered her junior year of high school last fall. But during the summer she changed her mind. What good did it do to learn things like history, algebra, and shorthand? She wanted to be free.

So, on the urging of her pot-smoking friends, she left home. Music was her life, so she took her guitar and bongo drums with her. She got a room in a shoddy, third-class hotel and started to work singing in a lounge outside the city limits. At last, she was free.

Her parents work in a small laundry. They did everything they could to persuade her to return home. They went to see her. They prayed. They contacted her minister. But she had no intention of ever returning to that prison. Since she had a well-proportioned body, men (most of them married) gave her big tips. In return, she learned to give herself. It was fun.

Exciting. Afterwards she would return to her grungy room and cry. But she was free

Her friends were on drugs. First it was pot and speed. But that was kid stuff. It wasn't too long before some of her friends introduced her to coke. And then to horse. She began to mix it with witchcraft and a little lesbianism. That was really swinging high.

Then she lost her job at the bar. She looked around for her men friends, but they had gone home to be with their wives. Her girl friends were worse off than she was. She called her parents and begged for money. They cried over the phone and pleaded with her to come home. But they refused to give her money for drugs. She slammed down the phone, cursing. She didn't need them. She was free.

She came by my house but chickened out before she rang the doorbell. She left a note in the mailbox. She was leaving town. Three dudes had promised her a good singing job in New York City. Would I please go by the laundry and see her parents? Please tell them she loved them and was sorry she had caused them pain. She'd be back after she got her head on straight.

I went to her hotel room. She was sitting on the side of the sagging bed. Her clothes, packed in a brown grocery bag, were near the door. A huge Janis Joplin poster leered down from the wall. An American flag, scrawled with hideous pictures of demons, was draped across the back of a chair. One corner had been dipped in blood, probably during a meeting of the witches' coven. The ashtray was filled with rancid marijuana butts. Her teeth were rotting. Her once beautiful face was lined and haggard.

I bit my lip. This dingy, cracked-plaster hotel room was a microcosm for a whole generation of kids rebelling against authority—kids dying for reality but looking in the wrong places.

I stood in the door, looking down at her. "I feel like I'm ninety," she said. "Some dude gave me the clap. I've gotta stop by the health clinic to get my V.D. shots."

She was the same age as my teenage daughter, but she talked like a burned-out street whore.

"H-h-how are my parents?" she stammered.

It was no time to mince words. "Heartbroken. They'd give their lives if you would return home."

"Sunday's mom's birthday," she said as though she hadn't heard me. "Would you go by and tell her I love her?" Suddenly the tears flowed profusely.

I shook my head slowly. "I'll not lie for you. If you really meant it, you'd go home and tell her yourself."

She blew her nose loudly and wiped it on a corner of the filthy bedspread.

"You don't understand. Home is prison for me. They'd want me to go back to school. To church. . . ."

Three skinny, sunken-chested dudes appeared in the hall outside the door. One had on no shirt. All had long, matted hair and scraggly beards. "Come on, chicky," one said. "New York is calling."

She gave me a pathetic look in which I saw the pleadings of an entire generation. "I've got to be free," she said.

"Like a plucked flower," I answered softly. "You're free only to die."

She picked up her stuff and walked past me, following the boys down the hall. She never looked back.

That was a year ago. Last Sunday night I saw her in the back row at church. She had aged twenty years, yet beneath the thick makeup I saw something else

During the offering she got out of her seat and started silently toward the front. A thousand eyes followed her slow progress. She was weeping. Two high school kids got up and walked with her. Half a dozen others joined them. By the time she reached the altar rail, there were fifty kids around her—some crying, others laughing. All loving her back to God.

19. Cadillac Christians

It was November and I sat cross-legged on the packed cow dung floor of a tiny hut in a Chitwan Tharu tribal village in Nepal. The natives had killed a bony old rooster in our honor. They served him—all of him—in a yellow and greenish mixture of rice and herbs. Fortunately it was extremely dark in the dung hut and we could not see what we were eating as we shoveled it, with our fingers, into our mouths.

The three Americans in the group—and I was one of them—did a lot of joking and laughing. We had to—just to keep from gagging. We asked God to "bless every bite" and claimed the Scripture in Mark 16 about eating poison. But you see, we could joke because we knew that in a few hours we'd be back in the mission plane on our way to Kathmandu. And the following week we'd be back in the promised land of America.

Halfway through the meal I looked up at the tiny, half-naked shriveled woman who had prepared our food. I could barely see her face in the dim light of the hut, but it was aglow with love. It had cost her family a month's wages to prepare this "feast" in our honor—and here we were laughing.

Suddenly I didn't see a simple tribal woman with a ring in her nose. I saw Mary pouring out the perfume on the feet of Jesus. I saw the widow dropping her mite into the treasury while Christ watched from the shadows. That dark-skinned, bare-footed woman had been touched by the hand of God. She was rich beyond measure. While I, who was about to fly back to my two-story house in Florida, was a pauper by comparison.

I let my mind drift back to my visit in a swamp slum in Bangkok the week before. We were being escorted by the wife of an Australian missionary and after we returned to the van it was obvious the young woman was badly shaken. And who wouldn't be? The conditions were indescribable. Tiny hovels of scraps of tar paper and bamboo thatch. When it rained, as it had in torrents those last few days, the people simply sat and shivered like animals in the forest. The children waded through mud and feces to the little shack provided by the Catholics and World Vision as a school. Even there, though, the drinking water in the large clay pots was filled with twisting worms and amoebae.

We sat silently in the van, waiting for the rest of the party to slog their way out of the swamp. After a long silence, the young missionary wife said, to no one in particular, "It makes you grateful for where you were born."

The pretty Thai nurse, who had accompanied us into the watery hell, answered softly. "Yes, I'm grateful I was born here in Thailand."

I wanted to weep. Had the missionary not said it, I am sure I would have—and branded myself as the Western chauvinist I actually am.

Unfortunately, we Americans have a way of equating financial prosperity with spiritual righteousness. Our big churches, great crusade meetings, million-dollar budgets, and the God-is-blessing-us-because-we-had-a-thousand-people-in-church-yesterday syndrome seems to have replaced the spirit of the One who had no place to lay His head.

It was Francis McNutt, a soft-spoken Dominican priest, who remarked at one of the recent World Conferences on the Holy Spirit in Jerusalem, "If Jesus were on earth He couldn't attend this conference. He wouldn't have the money—that is, unless He were invited as a speaker."

Everyone laughed. Again I wanted to cry.

One of my Southern Baptist friends says the two primary questions at the Monday morning ministers' meeting are "Jahave?" and "Jaget?" How many did jahave in church yesterday? How much money did jaget? That too is hilarious—if you can stop weeping long enough to laugh.

It's almost as sad as the common practice among Christian leaders of giving preference to the rich and famous. "Sit thou here in a good place—on the platform, in the best hotel, up in first class—and maybe you'll throw me a sop in return." (When was the last time you heard a sermon on James 2:1-18 or 5:1-11?)

The most shocking revelation American Christians can receive is that it is possible to be supernaturally prospered by God and still be out of His will. We have a way of equating prosperity with God's approval, which is why a church can persecute Spirit-baptized believers and still enjoy a huge budget and a ripe harvest of new members.

How can this be? Well, because God lets it rain on the just and the unjust. He loves His persecutors just as much as He loves those who love Him. And He blesses His Word—even when spoken by a jackass.

Americans, lest they forget, need to remember the wilderness of Sinai. Here three million Jews were protected and provided for by God for forty years. There was manna from heaven, protection from snakes, water from rocks, and clothes that never wore out. Yet they had missed God's divine intent for an entire generation. They were a dying people.

The blessing of God cannot be equated with Cadillacs or even three meals a day. It comes only as Christ transforms the inner person into a creature of love, joy, and peace. It's available for all, even if you live in a cow dung hut.

20. Formula for Peace

There seems to be built into every one of us the need for rest. Unlike animals who never take vacations, who never turn aside for pleasure or recreation, those of us in Adam's race are created not only for work—but for rest.

Throughout the Bible there are references to such things as "resting in the Lord," and the "Sabbath rest." The word includes freedom from oppression by the enemy, and peace of spirit, as well as the ordinary meanings such as relaxing our muscles and catching our breath.

This brings this entire concept of balancing our work-a-day week with a day of rest, of taking time off for an annual vacation, into a new perspective.

Dallas Albritton, who practices law in Tampa, recently returned from a vacation in Switzerland. While he was there he began asking himself why it was that Switzerland had been blessed across the years as a nation that had invariably escaped war. Even while the two great world wars were raging all around it, little Switzerland remained neutral—unscratched and unbombed. The natural explanation is that it is inaccessible, too mountainous for anyone to want it. Yet Austria, northern Italy, and parts of Germany and France are just as much alpine country as Switzerland—and they suffered heavily during the wars. Not only that, they have been constantly fighting with each other for centuries.

Dallas's interesting conclusion came on a Sunday morning while he was relaxing in his chateau overlooking a quaint little Swiss village. Starting about dawn and on up until mid-morning, he wrote in a letter, the valley was filled with the ringing of church bells calling the people to worship. Not only that, he said, but it was impossible to find a single shop open on the Lord's Day. They all rested—and observed the Sabbath in their own way.

He related this to a passage of Scripture hidden away in the 17th chapter of Jeremiah where God promises peace and prosperity to those who keep His Sabbath—and violence to those who choose to pollute it with work.

Interesting.

I tried this argument on another friend recently and he countered by saying, "But look at the Jews. They keep the Sabbath and tithe their incomes, yet they are constantly at war." True. Yet, despite the best efforts of man to eradicate them from the face of the earth, they are still here—and prospering—while their enemies have long since been consumed.

So, for these reasons as well as others of a practical nature, I am now looking forward with new dedication to set aside one day in seven as special unto the Lord. He made us for rest. I enjoy snuggling into His pattern.

21. Truth Revealed

It was our last Sunday in the mountains and the family decided to go to church. I say the family decided. Actually Jackie and I decided for them, and the children reluctantly agreed. They much preferred to have "church" on the front porch as we had the Sunday before.

We arrived late, as usual, and came in the back way. After getting lost and wandering through some musty halls (churches always assume visitors automatically know where to go), I finally swallowed my pride and asked directions. A little girl took us in tow—all six of us—led us up a flight of stairs and pointed to a door that opened onto a side balcony.

We walked in and were face to face with six hundred people—all staring at us. The kids panicked and tried to back out, but a friendly usher pulled us in and escorted us to the only vacant seats in the balcony. I wondered at the time why a block of six seats were empty when all the others were filled. I learned *why* the moment we sat down.

"What kind of church is this?" my teenage Tim asked. "A listening church?"

So that's the reason those seats were vacant. They were in a blind spot. We couldn't see the platform, the minister, even the choir. All we could do was listen. I whispered down the row of kids, seated between me and their mother. "Can you see?" All heads were shaking, all faces unhappy. I knew what they were thinking. We should have stayed on the porch at home.

At least we can sing, I thought. That was a mistake too. Following John Wesley's rules printed in the front of the hymn book, I sang "lustily" when the first hymn was announced. Halfway through the first stanza I noticed the couple in front of me were nudging each other with their elbows. As we started the second stanza, I distinctly heard them giggle.

Nothing takes the lust out of lusty singing as much as having someone giggle at you. Red-faced, I faded out and sort of hummed along. When I did, I realized that even though the congregation was standing with hymn books open and mouths moving, nobody was singing—at least not much. I soon realized this was indeed a "listening church" and joined the gang, moving my mouth and making growling, off-key noises.

The couple in front of me relaxed. The threat had disappeared. I looked down the row at the kids. They had been right. We should have stayed on the porch. At least there we could sing to our hearts' delight and disturb no one but the chipmunks.

After several responsive readings—more open books, moving mouths, and growls—we finally got to the sermon. This consisted of an unseen voice coming up out of an unknown space over the balcony rail. I had to simply assume there was someone down there doing the speaking. It looked like a lost morning.

Then I saw him—directly across from me in the opposite blind spot in the balcony on the far side of the room. He was leaning forward on the front edge of his pew, listening intently. White hair, full white mustache, wrinkled hands, white cane between his knees.

His eyes could not see, but his ears were hanging on every sermonic word. I could not stop looking at his expressive face as he nodded, smiled, and frowned in response to the sermon. On one occasion he even raised his hand in a grand gesture of approval. I watched, fascinated, as the message of the morning came alive in the expressive face of an old blind man. Far more effective than seeing the source of the sermon, I was seeing the result.

I left the service strengthened, helped, uplifted. Maybe that's what going to church is all about, anyway—seeing in one another the result of truth proclaimed.

22. I Wish I Had Said It As Well

It was noon, but the airport at Alexandria, Louisiana, was still fogged in. As the ticket agent announced the last plane of the day had just flown over, unable to land, an audible groan went up from the passengers, many of whom had been waiting since dawn.

Although most of the people in the terminal were trying to get to New Orleans and points east, I was on my way to Los Angeles. Fortunately, I had not yet checked in my rental car, so I decided to run the chance of driving up to Shreveport, hoping the fog would lift and I could make connections with a night flight into Dallas and on to L.A.

While I was checking the schedule with the ticket agent, I was interrupted by a tap on my shoulder. A young man, dressed in the traditional Amish garb of black suit and white shirt with no tie, asked if he could ride with me. Three others, standing close by, heard our conversation and asked if they could join us. In minutes I had a full car and we were carrying bags out of the terminal, stuffing them into the trunk.

It was quite a group. Karl, the young Amish fellow with a thick neck and bulging arm and shoulder muscles under his simple homespun black coat, was a Pennsylvania blacksmith. One of a vanishing breed, he confessed he disliked flying, but had to make an emergency trip to Louisiana to see his ailing mother. It was his first time away from Pennsylvania, but he seemed at peace. He was now trying to get back to Harrisburg.

Flo was a lady bartender from Shreveport who had flown down the night before to settle a deal on a house that one of her ex-husbands had willed her. Fiftyish, with a loud, raspy voice caused by too many cigarettes, I could sense she could hold her own in any kind of encounter. I chuckled under my breath as she crawled on the small back seat and adjusted her girdle around her ample midriff, all the while muttering a few choice words about things in general.

The other two men, who squeezed into the back seat with her, said they were preachers. One of them was stocky with wide eyes and bushy hair. His job, he said, as we took turns in the car introducing ourselves, was to convert sinners. His companion, who kept muttering "Amen," was his business manager. They were from the same town in Oklahoma and were on the last leg of an evangelistic campaign which had taken them through five states in the southeast.

We had barely gotten out on the highway when things went bad. Flo pulled out her cigarettes and started to light up. The preacher objected. It was bad enough being cramped into the tiny back seat of a car without having to breathe her smoke. Inside I was grateful she put her weeds away, but wished the preacher had used a little more tact and gentleness.

But the preacher didn't let it lie. In almost the same breath he launched into a frontal attack on the evils of tobacco. We still had 180 miles to go and already had a full-scale battle going on in the back seat. It was the young, bull-necked Amish fellow in the front seat who set things right, however.

Turning around in his seat, he looked at the Bible-quoting crab in the back and said very quietly, very matter-of-factly, "Friend, I am a peace-loving man. I detest physical violence. But you are using the Bible as a club and I do not appreciate it. Furthermore, you are insulting a woman for whom Christ died. Now I suggest you move your mouth to one side, for I am about to plant my fist where your lips are now flapping."

There was immediate silence in the car. I wanted to cheer but held my peace. When we stopped for gas, the young blacksmith apologized for his loss of control. The preachers accepted it, but said they thought they would make better time if they took the bus. No one objected and once back in the car, Flo lit up and chain-smoked the rest of the way to Shreveport. I knew Karl was having as much trouble breathing as I, but he didn't seem to mind. In fact, he and Flo spent most of the time engaged in deep conversation.

When we parted at the airport, it was Flo who reached over, touched his arm, and asked him to remember her in prayer.

Karl may be a blacksmith, but he also knows something about farming. I have a feeling the seed he planted in Louisiana will someday grow into a tree that bears fruit.

23. *Riding Off in All Directions*

After years of cramped subdivision living, we finally moved into a new house in the country. But, unlike intelligent people, we didn't move all at once. Only after having lived in the new house for more than three months did we move the last of our belongings out of the old house. During these three months I lived in limbo, accomplishing little.

There are some things you should do all at once. And moving, like ripping a piece of adhesive tape off a hairy leg, is one of them.

The difference between the achiever and the underachiever is focus. Jesus said the Christian should learn to concentrate on one thing. The double-minded man who tries to live in too many worlds (or too many houses) never reaches his potential. He becomes like a friend of mine who is an expert in nine different areas—from engineering to theology—but never has been able to hold a job down for more than six months.

THE LAST WORD

Lip affections are particularly disastrous. No man can serve two masters, be loyal to two women, or live in two houses.

I look around at the people who are achieving and notice all of them have learned the secret of focus. They have learned to say no to the trivial and yes to the important. They have learned to shut out all but the priority issues of life. Like Paul, they forget those things which are past and press on toward the mark of their high calling.

The major difference between a river and a swamp is that the river is going one place while the swamp tries to go everywhere. The river has a goal: reaching the sea. The swamp, though, rebels against the discipline of riverbanks (Hallelujah! I'm free from the law!) and remains a constant underachiever, producing only undesirable things like snakes and mosquitoes. (Although it may do a lot of bragging about the territory it covers.)

It's not a sin to be a one-talent person. The sin lies in wanting to do ten things with your one talent, and getting so frustrated that you wind up achieving nothing at all.

24. *The Field of the Slothful*

The first week of vacation in our mountain cabin in North Carolina is usually spent fixing things.

Last year it was the stone wall that needed fixing. The wall is almost four hundred feet long and runs the length of the curving driveway from the country road up to the cabin on the hillside.

The wall was built more than twenty years ago by our across-the-knoll-neighbor, Clem Sumner. Clem has lived in these parts all his life. His pappy used to own much of the land on the far side of the mountain and Clem is related to most of the people in the valley.

I can remember, as a child, how Clem used to meet us at the train station with a horse and wagon. That was back during World War II, and my mother and the children would ride the train from Vero Beach to Hendersonville to spend the summer, leaving daddy at home with the one car to run the business and perform his duties as chief air raid warden for Indian River

County.

Clem was a dependable, lovable storyteller who never seemed to be able to do enough to help around our summer cabin. "Jest tell me what to do, Miz B," he would say, chewing on a straw with his hat cocked back on his head and his thumbs in the bib of his overalls.

It was during this time that Clem, an expert stonemason, built the wall. I had never seen such beautiful, flat stones as he dragged up the road, using a ground sled behind his horse. He called them "creek rock," but I now recognize them as flint, granite, and assorted shades of sandstone filled with tiny specks of mica which glitter in the sunlight like thousands of tiny gems.

Across the years, though, the water has eroded the soil behind the wall. During the winter it collected in pockets and froze, loosening the mortar. Thrift, a hanging vegetation which grows along the top of the wall and blooms beautifully in the early spring, had sent its roots into the crevices, and finally some of the stones had toppled forward into the ditch.

One morning I set out to repair the wall. After spending the last two months doing nothing more strenuous than punching keys on a typewriter, I looked forward to the manual labor. Mixing the concrete in a wheelbarrow, picking up a rivet hammer and trowel, I set off down the driveway like Nehemiah returning from Babylon to repair the wall around Jerusalem. I chipped away the old concrete, reshaped the stones with the rivet hammer, slapped the new mortar into place, and tenderly replaced the stones.

But it was a sad job, for Clem wasn't there to help. Like the wall, Clem had broken down. Alcohol had eroded his life, crumbling the weak mortar of his flesh. Instead of a lovable, dependable man, he had become mean and dangerous, stalking the mountains with his shotgun, threatening to kill those who crossed his path.

I remembered the words of Solomon as I worked. "I went by

the field of the slothful . . . and it was all grown over with thorns . . . and the stone wall thereof was broken down."

Life is full of Clems. Creative experts, toppled forward into the ditches of wastefulness. Only the Master Stonemason can repair the wall of Clem's life, and the process is always the same: chipping, reshaping, and replacing. Even then, it can only be done when the wall yields itself to the Master's hammer and trowel.

25. Mistaken Identity

For a number of years now, I have fancied myself to be a unique individual. When I go into a strange city, I enjoy flipping through the phone book to see if I can find another Jamie Buckingham. So far I have never found one, which is a good thing. I don't know what I would do if I did. But all this simply lends weight to the fact that there are no others like me.

I enjoy my uniqueness. It gives me a sense of independence and freedom. Being me, and not having to be anyone else, means I don't have to imitate or meet someone else's standards (except God's, who has a way of constantly holding me accountable). There is no freedom that matches the freedom of knowing who you are, knowing you are one of a kind, a special breed that fits no other mold.

However, this fantasy was shot down recently when I made a quick weekend trip to Charlotte, North Carolina. It was the weekend of the World 600, a famous sports event in which red-necked men with heavy sideburns climb into unbelievably expensive, precision-made automobiles and chase each other around an oval track at speeds that take your breath away. Frankly, I prefer to get my kicks from other sources than sitting in the broiling sun for five hours listening to cars go varoom, varoom, and hoping some drunk won't vomit on my shoes. Unfortunately, a lot of other people think otherwise, and most of them had migrated to Charlotte for the race.

My two sons were with me as I checked into a local motel. Even though the race was the next afternoon, a lot of the fans had already started celebrating and by 9:00 P.M. there was as much noise at the motel as there would be at the race track the next afternoon. The Richard Petty Fan Club was just across the patio and those who weren't in their rooms drinking and shouting were racing their cars in and out of the driveway going varoom, varoom just like the real guys do. It was at this point that I realized I was no longer uniquely me.

For some reason, when I am viewed from a particular angle (especially if the viewer is slightly inebriated) I look exactly like a racing driver named Cale Yarborough. A red-necked friend of mine had once mentioned that, but I had laughed him off. In Charlotte it was no laughing matter.

I was just returning from the Coke machine with a bucket of ice when one of the Richard Petty fans spotted me. "There's old Cale," he shouted to his drunk friends. "Let's do Richard a favor and go break his fingers."

I decided this was no time to try to explain I was just a unique guy who lives in Florida and drives a '67 Volkswagen. I quickly vanished into my room and, to my boys' delight, huddled behind the curtains while the drunks ran up and down the sidewalk shouting, "Where's old Cale? We wanna break his fingers."

A friend of mine says if he's ever mistaken for anyone, he hopes it's Jesus. I haven't had the heart to tell him that if that's the case they won't just break his fingers, they'll nail him to a cross. But he's right, you know. If you're going to get beat up, it's far better being mistaken for Jesus than some race car driver whose followers sit around going "varoom, varoom."

26. Giving God My Junk

Charles Simpson once said the two happiest days of his life were the day he bought his boat—and the day he sold it.

Unfortunately, I didn't believe him. I bought one of my own.

First it was a new prop when my son hit some rocks in the river. Then it was a new crankshaft. Last summer the boat and trailer came loose from a friend's truck and wound up in the show window of a furniture store. That meant a new hull plus the plateglass window and a bunch of bent lawn chairs. Last month the cylinders needed reboring and the battery died.

Definition: "Boat: a hole in the water into which a fool pours his money."

The boat was obviously a jinx. I began to think about giving it to the church. That way I could count it as a contribution and escape having to give my tithe in cash.

Somehow, though, that smacked of the time I tried to trade in my old car for a newer model. I asked the dealer if he would give me a better price if I included a used set of tires in the bargain.

"Why should I want your junk?" he asked.

It's disturbing that I often wait until a thing is almost beyond repair—or out of control—before I give it to God.

Recently a young missionary family moved into our church. The people provided most of the furnishings for their house. Everything but the refrigerator. That night at the dinner table I had a generous idea.

"Our old refrigerator is on its last legs. Why don't we give it to Paul and Ginny and buy ourselves a new one—with an automatic icemaker?"

"You mean," my discerning wife smiled, "why not give God our leftovers?"

"Yeah, dad," our teenaged Bonnie chimed in, "I thought God was supposed to get the first fruits—not the rotten apples at the bottom of the barrel."

Unfortunately, I'm like the little kid who took two dimes to church—one for the offering and the other for an ice cream cone. When he dropped one coin down the gutter in front of the church, he said, "Sorry, God, there goes your dime."

We still have our old refrigerator. God's servants have a new one—with an automatic icemaker.

You see, the old me is always trying to work out some kind of a "deal" with God. Last year I spoke at a prayer retreat in North Carolina. The day I arrived I promised the Lord I would give all the honorarium (I expected it to be small) to my friend Aley Gonzalez, a native pastor in the Philippines. I felt really good about it until they handed me the check. It was for $3,000.

Hmmm, I thought. Had I known it was going to be this big I would have promised God half—and kept the rest. But something (or Someone) told me God's words to Moses were still in effect: "That which has gone out of thy mouth I will require of you." It seemed better to keep my promise than to have God extract it from me.

Bonnie was right. God wants our best—not our junk, leftovers, and compromised promises.

Anyway, I would have looked silly trying to get that boat down the aisle of the church.

27. Miss Henrietta

Love is not limited by age, just as it is not limited by race, education, or how much money one has.

For thirty years Ed Seymour was the town drunk in Greenwood, South Carolina. His wife, Henrietta, twelve years his senior, stayed with him through those three decades of hell. If anyone ever knew the meaning of the biblical term "longsuffering," it was Miss Henrietta.

After Mr. Ed stopped drinking he exchanged his bottle for a Bible. I don't mean he became a preacher. He didn't quit his job as a newspaper distributor. He just became what a Christian ought to be.

It became a daily occurrence for Mr. Ed to pull up to our back door in his ancient car, filled with back issues of the *Greenville News* and the *Atlanta Journal*, load up all five of our children (including the baby who could barely toddle), and take them around town distributing his papers. They invariably wound up in one of the cafes on the town square where Mr. Ed would drink coffee while the children ate ice cream.

Mr. Ed died after we left Greenwood and moved back to Florida. Part of us died with him. Only Miss Henrietta remained. Even though she was old and wrinkled and had no children of her own, our children maintained the relationship. They called regularly on the phone, and at least once a year spent a week visiting in the old frame two-story house on Oakhaven Court. Like Miss Henrietta, the house belonged to another era. It needed painting badly. The door to the one bathroom wouldn't close. The linoleum on the kitchen floor was peeling back and the plaster on the high ceilings was dropping to the floor, leaving the wooden laths exposed. But the old house, and the old woman who lived there, were very special in our lives.

Unlike Mr. Ed, who died a lingering death, Miss Henrietta went suddenly. It was Christmas and the neighbor who called said her heart just gave out. The flow of liquor at Christmas had always been a temptation for Mr. Ed—even after he stopped drinking. From a desire born out of years of suffering, she knew Christmas was the one time of year she needed to be with him most. I think that's part of the reason she gave in so readily.

But with Miss Henrietta's passing, passed also the children's reason to return to Greenwood, the place where most of them were born. Gone were the chickens that roosted in the trees behind the house. Gone were the old cars. Gone was the little red bicycle that sat on the front porch, waiting Sandy's visit. In fact, it wasn't long before the old house would be gone, too, torn down to make room for a new parking lot.

We sat up late the night Miss Henrietta died. There was no need to return to Greenwood for the funeral, but we needed to talk. The children huddled in the big bed with us as we cried together, prayed together, and talked of life and change. I remembered the time when I returned to Florida and found my parents had moved out of the big house, the house where I had been raised, into a much smaller place. I loved that big house. I knew every room, every squeak of the walls, every secret hiding place. But it had to go if I was to learn the meaning of Isaiah's statement that everything material disappears. Only God, and God's love which we find through our old friends, remains. And in time, they too—like Mr. Ed and Miss Henrietta—depart. Leaving only God. And memories.

The next morning I got a call from the high school. It was the secretary asking us to come pick up our fifteen-year-old Bonnie who was in the office crying. I went for her and then we drove around for a while. Finally she looked up through her tears and said, "I told them my grandmother had died. Is that all right?"

"I think Miss Henrietta would like that," I answered. Like I said. Love is not limited by age.

28. A Day in the Hammock

I spent one entire day last week lying in a hammock. Vacation was drawing to a close and I had spent almost no time doing nothing—which is what vacations are for. So last Sunday morning I got up late, took the big Pawleys Island woven rope hammock off the porch and strung it between two black oak trees near the green pasture. It was a lazy morning. The clouds were still on the mountains and even at nine o'clock, dawn was having to struggle to arrive. Checking the chains around the trunks of the trees to make sure they were secure, and accompanied by several books, I eased my body into the stretchy weave and with hands under my head, murmured a prayer of thanksgiving to a God who knew my need and had commanded me to "come ye apart and rest awhile."

It was a delicious feeling, swaying gently in the cool mountain breeze. I realized I was indulging myself, much as a man might take an entire evening just to sit before a roaring log fire, sip wine, and munch cheese. It was the same feeling I had occasionally when I would stretch out on the floor and let my wife scratch my back: "Oh, that feels good. . . a little to the left. . . um, that's right, now back to the center. . . ahhh, scratch right there. Don't ever stop."

And so I indulged myself in the hammock. All day long.

The children drove into town for church services. Jackie sat on the porch of the cabin struggling through all those rabbits in *Watership Down*. And I lay in the hammock, looking up at the canopy of green leaves splashed against the blue sky, and did nothing.

Man is the only species on earth given to reflection. Yet most of us, preferring to treat ourselves like beasts of burden, work so hard we never have time to stop and reflect. Vivid on my mind was the experience of a week before as I followed my daddy and mother through busy O'Hare Airport in Chicago. Two young skycaps were pushing their wheelchairs as they rushed to catch the plane to Rochester, Minnesota, and Mayo Clinic. I was too busy to do much thinking then, but now, in the hammock, I reflected on Shakespeare's concept that all the world's a stage with exits and entrances, and how in the last act we return to the first and become again helpless as babes, dependent on others. And I remembered that moment at O'Hare when the wheelchairs passed the young couple pushing baby strollers. One man in his time does play many parts, but I disagree with Shakespeare that we have to exit in "second childishness and mere oblivion." Not so. Even though we may exit sans teeth and sans eyes, we are still noble creatures of God, just a little lower than the angels and redeemed under the blood of Christ. Wheelchairs and canes, perhaps, but we are still noble creatures with dominion over all the earth.

It was a good conclusion and one I might not have grasped had I not taken time to spend the day in the hammock, reflecting. Oh, there were many other things, some too impossible to relate, but they all tasted good as I let them run through my relaxed mind.

Every man needs four things in his life: two trees, a woven rope hammock, and time to use it. God will supply the rest.

29. Can a Pack Rat Get to Heaven?

A wise man once suggested we should take inventory every two months and discard everything not used during that period of time. It's a valid spiritual principle. When God moves and beckons us to follow, we need to travel light. Not burdened by things of this world.

But what do you do when you have a whole room full of things that might come in handy one day?

About every two years, we are forced to clean out the back room of our house, which is tantamount to going through the Smithsonian Institution and deciding what to keep and what to throw away. Our back room, which we affectionately call the "junk room," is part utility, part workshop, and part storage hole. It usually takes about two years for the junk to begin to take over the living area of our house. It spreads, like cinchbugs in the grass, encroaching first into the den, then into the kitchen, and finally onto the dining room table. If we don't do something, we would eventually have to move out of the house. So, every so often, I declare "operation throwaway."

But what do you do with odds and ends that you never have used but just might need one of these days? For instance, we have a mayonnaise jar filled with assorted keys. To my knowledge, they don't fit any lock in the house, but you never can tell. . . .

Then there are the electric train sets. True, all the tracks are different gauges and the transformers are burned out. But one of these days electric trains will be antiques and perhaps my children would like to show them to their children (no doubt so they could put them in their junk room).

From surplus sales I've acquired aluminum cooking sets, cartons of canned heat, water purifiers, and salt pills. All so far unused. And I think GI pants, the ones with the big pockets on the sides, are the greatest. I once bought six pair during a closeout sale. All are too small now, but I keep telling myself that one day there'll be no more war and they won't make swell pants like this any more. In the meantime, I had better hold onto them.

I never wear a hat, but you never can tell when . . . maybe someday I might play that old concertina again . . . and everybody saves *National Geographics*, don't they? I'll bet my son can hardly wait to get his hands on a beer mug inscribed Mercer University, 1954, ATO. And a man never knows when he might need a broken phonograph and a big, long cardboard box filled with bent curtain rods.

It's like the old clothes in my closet. I just can't bear to throw them away. I know the style has changed since the fifties, but one of these days I might lose a lot of weight and be able to slip back into them again. I can always use them on camping trips—in case we ever go camping.

I remembered reading about a man who never threw anything away. He stored it all in his attic and one day, you guessed it, his house collapsed on top of him.

Can a Pack Rat Get to Heaven?

My wife reminded me that last summer we took a long vacation and lived happily out of a suitcase for almost six weeks. If I could get along without that old commando machete and those five pair of holey tennis shoes then, I could surely get along without them now. I bit my lip, closed my eyes, and threw away everything I hadn't used in two months—including the 1954 beer mug and an old ammunition belt.

That evening, sitting quietly in the den, I heard a terrible commotion in the junk room. Opening the door, I saw my two teenage children carting stuff from the garage bin back into the house.

"Gosh, dad," my son said with a look of dismay on his face, "one day these old electric trains will be antiques. . . ." I closed the door and returned to the TV. Like father like son. I have bred another generation of pack rats, and I suspect they will have just as much trouble squeezing through the eye of a needle with all that junk, as Jesus' proverbial camel.

30. Plugged In

In my writing studio, in my Florida house, I have an electric typewriter. If I were to come in one morning and flip the switch and not hear the familiar whirr, I would immediately look to see if my machine were plugged in. I wouldn't sit in my chair in front of the keyboard and wail, "Oh, electricity, please come into my typewriter and make it work."

Nor would I bow my head in pious prayer and plead, "God, in the name of Jesus, fill my typewriter with power."

No, I would simply plug the cord into the socket which is the outlet for power, which in turn is connected to the source of power, and wait for the machine to begin to hum. Then I would go to work typing.

The entire universe is filled with the healing power of God. But in order to be healed, one has to come in contact with that power—he has to be touched by that power. Simply sitting around staring at the socket is not sufficient. To get the power from the source to the need, you have to be plugged in. God is the source of the power. Jesus Christ, God's Son, is the outlet of that power. And the Holy Spirit is the conductor which carries the power to the need.

God has made a world that is run by laws, His laws. There are laws of nature, gravity, physics, chemistry, sound and light. But there is another law—the law of love and grace—which supersedes all other laws. And when God invokes this law, that is, when He intervenes in the affairs of men personally, we call it a miracle. But to God such healings are just as "natural" as an apple falling downward when it drops from a tree.

Dr. Alexis Carrel, physician and scientist, declares that he has seen skin cancer disappear at the command of faith. But that is not breaking the laws of nature. It is the superimposition of a higher law.

A couple of years ago I accidentally shoved the point of a screwdriver through my hand. With blood squirting everywhere, I sat down on the kitchen floor, grabbed the wound with my other hand, and began praying quietly in the Spirit, using the prayer language which had been given me a short time before. In less than five minutes the wound had healed. Miracle? Surely! But when viewed from God's side, it was merely the result of one of His children who had been willing to plug himself into the source of power.

There are millions of Christians who have died of disease whom God longed to heal. Occasionally God will reach out and heal us even though we do not ask for it. But by and large God works (and we see His perfect example in the healing, miracle ministry of Jesus) by waiting for His children to put themselves in a healing posture. He has provided, in the person of His Holy Spirit, the healing agent. All we have to do is reach out and be touched by Him. Or, on some occasions, have someone who is filled with Him touch us for Him. But in all cases, Jesus is the healer, and the Holy Spirit is the conductor who brings the power to us.

Plug yourself in, my friend. Let the power flow through you—and be healed.

31. The Call of Plush Carpets

His name was Paul Mansfield. When he graduated from medical school his professors predicted he would become one of the great surgeons of the world. They were right—but they didn't know just *how* right they were.

After graduation he turned down a partnership with a distinguished physician and moved to a desolate little village in the coal mining region of Appalachia. The only doctor in a fifty-mile radius, he opened a small office in a room over the town's one dry goods store. For forty years, he ministered to the poor, living and working out of his office above the store.

He delivered babies in hovels where even the animals shivered in the cold. He extracted tonsils, set broken limbs, and sutured cuts—often without the aid of basic drugs. He diagnosed disease, performed minor operations, and referred when necessary to the big city hospital fifty miles away. He helped the aged, comforted the incurables, tended the dying, and suffered through many a long, cold night with anxious loved ones.

Everyone was poor. Very poor. They paid him as they could, sometimes in produce, but most of the time not at all. But he was not working for a wage, but because he had received a "calling" to minister. His goal: to heal the sick.

When the flu epidemic struck the mountain area, he gave himself day after day—traveling from one mountain shack to another giving shots and antibiotics. There was little time for sleep, for as soon as he lay his weary head on the pillow in his upstairs office, there would be a knock at the door or the phone would ring. It wasn't long before he, too, became a victim of the flu.

His last conscious act was to call for his day book and across each account scribble "Paid in Full." Then he died.

People came from all over the mountains to attend his funeral. They even shut down the operations in the coal mines so the men could pay homage. The little white church was jammed with people. They stood outside the windows, the women in bonnets and the men holding little children on their shoulders—most of whom had been delivered by the country doctor.

Eight strong mountain men, looking strange in their mismatched coats and ties, carried the casket from the church. Placing it on their shoulders, they walked quietly down the mountain path to the country graveyard. Hundreds of people fell in step behind them, singing softly with tear-stained faces, "There's a land that is fairer than day . . . and by faith we shall see it afar. . . ."

They lowered the wooden box into the open grave, and then by common consent scattered far and wide. Each person returned with a stone which he placed on the grave. The mountain of rocks was shoulder high when the last stone was in place.

Then the country preacher stepped forward and laid the last object on the grave. It was the doctor's shingle that he had pulled off the pole in front of the dry goods store. It simply said, "Dr. Mansfield. Office Upstairs."

That was many years ago, but my aunt still remembers the story. Those same poor people still live in the mountains. Now they are without a doctor or a preacher. Perhaps the call of the plush office has more appeal than a simple wooden shingle that says, "Office Upstairs."

Yes, Lord

32. *Go National*

I keep having to remind myself that *achieving* is not nearly as important as *trying*. The reason I have to keep reminding myself is, I do a lot more trying than I do achieving.

A number of years ago I woke in the middle of the night having heard what I knew was the "voice of God." It was time, the voice said, to syndicate, on a national scale, the weekly newspaper column I had been writing for my hometown paper.

All signs were "go." My name appeared on the masthead of the largest religious magazine in the world and my weekly column had just received a first place award from the Florida Press Association. I was sure America's newspaper editors would be eager for my byline.

The next day, as I began making serious plans, I saw this could be God's way to get our financially strapped family out of debt. I would offer my material, not to the large daily papers, but to the more than five thousand weekly newspapers in

America—all of whom needed good writers. Besides this, I would give them a deal they couldn't refuse and offer my stuff for the ridiculously cheap price of five dollars per column. If only ten percent of the papers in the nation bought it, that would amount to twenty-five hundred dollars per week. A fortune!

The elders of the church agreed this was God's will. They were especially excited when I told them I would soon be able to support the church, rather than having the church support me. Who wouldn't confirm something as good as that. My fellow editors urged me on. My wife and children saw this as an opportunity to keep me home. Besides, this would be a family business. I could put the kids on salary and have them prepare the mailouts, lick the stamps, and count the money as it came rolling in.

I tried the big syndicates, but none of them were interested. That didn't dampen my spirits, however, for they would have taken half the loot anyway. Undaunted, since God had spoken, I determined to submit my material directly to the nation's papers myself.

I drained our children's educational account and spent more than fifteen hundred dollars additional money sending camera-ready samples, complete with stamped, return-addressed envelopes and a contract, to more than five thousand various editors. After six weeks of unbelievable hard work, two papers had accepted my offer—and one of them said they would pay only two dollars a column.

Three weeks later, these two dropped me. Broke and humiliated, I was a total failure as a syndicated columnist.

I wish I could report, years later, that I am now America's favorite syndicated columnist. That God had taken my failure and turned it into a marvelous victory. That the confirmation of my elders was valid. That the prophecy was really God, only I missed His perfect timing and had to wait. But I can't. Instead, the dream died in its place. I have a deep sense of satisfaction in doing what I am doing, without asking for more.

"But what about that voice which woke you in the night?" an intense friend asked. "Was it God? Or Satan?"

Looking back on it, I conclude the voice was neither. It was me. As a result, I have arrived at some interesting conclusions.

First, don't pray for humility unless you are prepared to be humiliated. That seems to be God's choice way to hurry up the process. I should have known this, after all, for when I had earlier prayed for patience, I received—you know—tribulation.

Second, anything that is done to earn money for God to use is foolhardy. God doesn't want our money. He just wants us. To go into business to support the Kingdom is tantamount to asking Rockefeller if he needs a loan.

I remember praying, as a young man, for one million dollars—and promising God I'd give Him ninety percent of it. It sounded spiritual until I examined my motives, which concluded that all I would get out of the deal was a hundred thousand dollars and that someone had already given God nine hundred thousand dollars and He didn't need any more—at least not in this tax year, anyway.

However, I am also convinced that achievement is not nearly as important as obedience. In other words, it's better to strike out than to sit, huddled fearfully, in the dugout, unwilling even to come to bat.

It's much like Peter's experience in water-walking. Every sermon I've ever heard on that subject deals with Peter's failure. Poor guy, if he had only kept his eyes on Jesus he never would have gone under. Good point. But at least he tried. The other fellows in the boat were all quaking behind the gunwales. The passing of the test, it seems, lies not in our ability to imitate Jesus, but in our willingness to try.

God does not intend for us to walk on water as a way of life (although there may be times when that is necessary). That sinking is far less a sin than never trying. God's call to us is to obey—and run the risk of being called a fool and a failure in the eyes of the world.

The crown of righteousness fits on a wet head just as easily as it does on a dry one.

33. Cocktail Chatter

The average American feels uncomfortable discussing spiritual things. We do pretty well when it comes to sports, business, politics, the weather, the Dow Jones, our children and the "good old days." But let someone bring up the subject of God, prayer, miracles, or Jesus Christ—and everyone gets a little fidgety.

I recently attended one of those before dinner "happy hours" in New York. Everyone was standing around with a cocktail glass talking about sports, business, politics, the weather, the Dow Jones, their children and the "good old days." I thought it was time to stop wasting time. I turned to the man nearest me, a nice looking fellow with a dark goatee and glasses, and said simply, "Do you ever pray?"

He swallowed his olive. Whole. In fact, I thought I was going to have to pray for him. He finally caught his breath and gasped, "Not very much." He then started coughing violently and walked quickly toward the bathroom.

Later we approached the buffet table and I got into a conversation with the couple behind me in line. We talked about sports, business, politics, the weather, the Dow Jones and finally got around to our children. Their kids, it seemed, were off in drugs. I thought I'd try again.

"Jackie and I pray for our kids. In fact, every night before they go to sleep I go to their bedrooms, lay hands on them, and pray out loud."

I suddenly realized everyone around us in line had grown quiet. All were listening. But when I looked up at them, they all quickly turned away. I turned back to the couple I had been talking to and they both were ghost white. "Have I offended you?" I asked innocently, knowing I hadn't offended them—I had just scared them speechless.

They mumbled something about not being "religious" and quickly moved through the serving line. I thought about the fellow who almost choked on his olive and wondered if he would have gotten "religious" if he thought he was going to die. Probably so. In a hurry, too.

That's the way we are. But I think I'll keep asking my little questions. Maybe someday, someone will answer me with tears in their eyes.

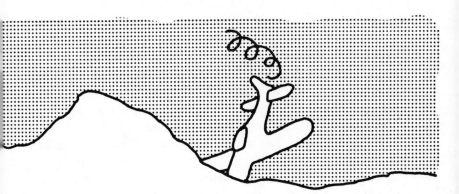

34. Hidden Meanings

Bruce Morgan spoke in our church one Sunday morning and said something which caused me to lay aside my Bible and reach for my notebook and pen.

"There is something too strong about truth for the human palate to receive all at once."

The reason, he said, was that truth always demands change. In fact, a full dose will actually put to death the old nature of man. Therefore, rather than accept pure truth we choose to water it down, stone our prophets, or even believe an outright lie if it makes things easier.

Artists, especially impressionist painters, choose to give us tidbits of truth hidden behind images, hoping a little will soak in and bring gradual change.

Novelists realize too much truth will cause the reader to reject their work; thus they build in "hidden meanings" to their stories.

Just so, every serious teacher, especially one who writes,

suffers the same frustrations. He has something to say which will change the lives of his readers. Yet he also understands that full exposure to the truth—especially if it cuts across the grain of some family tradition, financial motivation, or religious belief—will cause many of his readers to reject both his truth and him personally. Stones, hemlock, and crosses seem to accompany those who deal in truth with a capital T.

Therefore, many, like myself, are forced to give their readers little nuggets at a time, coating them with humor and imagery, hoping a little bit of sugar will make the medicine go down.

Jesus, who taught in parables, once told His disciples, "I have more I want to tell you, but you're unable to swallow it. You'd choke on it."

I thought about this recently as I read President Carter's energy crisis message. For years the experts have been telling us we're running out of fuel. Very few listened. Now the top man is also convinced. Yet despite his warnings, nothing has altered our extravagant way of living. In fact, if the president keeps pushing this controversial thesis, a lot of Americans will start plotting to get rid of him. We simply don't want to face reality, much less change.

Reports keep coming to us from places like South Africa, Rhodesia, Thailand, and the Philippines—not to mention Nepal, Italy, Ethiopia, and Argentina. Many nations are "on the brink" and could lose their freedom. But that's too much truth for those of us in free America to swallow. It's a retake of the way we rejected the warnings about Hungary, Czechoslovakia, and Poland.

Please, we cry out, stop confusing us with the facts.

I keep remembering Cy Roddenberry's story of boarding a Mexican airliner at the little airport in Veracruz. They taxied out to the end of the runway and then taxied back. There was a short wait and finally the airplane taxied back out and took off. Once they were airborne and over the rugged mountains, Cy called for the stewardess.

"What happened back there?"

"Oh, the pilot found something wrong with the engine and brought the plane back to the ramp. He said it was too dangerous to fly."

Alarmed, Cy looked out the window at the mountains far below and asked, "Did they change the engine?"

"Oh, no, senor," she smiled. "They changed the pilot."

There are a lot of things I would like to tell you—things which would change your life and bring you happiness and abundance. But they would call for death to your old way—even death to some of your religious practices. So, I come in parables, hoping you will go beyond them to seek the Truth for yourself.

The danger, of course, lies in inoculations. Some will catch just enough truth to keep them from getting infected with the real thing. Hopefully, though, you'll go beyond this book, beyond all books, even beyond—do I dare say it? Well, let the hymn-writer say it for me:

Beyond the sacred page I seek thee, Lord.

Now if the legalist fully understood those words, he would rip them from his hymnbook. So I must be careful. For too much truth could easily cause you to rip me, too. And I'm not ready to be kicked off the plane—at least not yet.

35. The Face of God

It was late at night as the wind blew through the North Carolina mountains where I was ensconced alone in my little cabin doing some serious writing. The trees bent in awesome majesty before it. Treetops swirled in the darkness, leaves blew, scattering before the wind like whipped school children before the headmaster, dead branches broke and tumbled to the earth—it was a wonderful sight.

I stood at the edge of the pasture, in the shadow of a towering white pine dark against the sky. The wind played across the tops of the rich green hay, causing it to bend and straighten, bend and straighten in fluid patterns. During the intermittent flashes of lightning I could see the yellow and white daisies and the fragile Queen Anne's lace which are sprinkled throughout the hay, nodding and bobbing in syncopated time with the flow of the music of the wind. The two ponies, sensing the excitement of the clashing of the elements, were standing on the hilltop, heads erect, manes blowing in the wind.

I leaned against the rough bark of a tough old red oak and listened to the thunder boom through the mountains. There was no rain, only brilliant streaks of lightning followed by the roar of thunder as it rumbled and rolled up one valley and down another. Unlike thunder in the flatlands where there is nothing to provide an echo, thunder in the mountains has character. It rolls on and on like an old carriage down a gravel road, up one valley and down another, sometimes seeming to grow in intensity as the mountains pick it up and hurl it back until it finally fades away in the distance.

Oddly, the dark forest around me was filled with the flickering lights of thousands of fireflies. Perhaps under the protection of the trees they were immune from the howling wind. I could see them across the pasture, also, in a small wooded area where there is a stand of towering poplars and hardwoods. The woods, dark and deep, were alive with the tiny, flashing lights. It was a magnificent sight, the wind blowing the tall hay, the trees bending and swaying, the lightning behind the mountains and the woods alive with glittering lights. No theater marquee or Broadway lights could compare with the beauty of this panorama.

I came inside the cabin and lit the kerosene lamp. The harsh glare of electric light would have utterly destroyed the mood of the moment. The reflections of the lamp danced across the walls and ceiling, keeping time with the howling wind outside the window. I lay for a long time on top of the covers, listening, watching. In the sounds of nature there is manna for the soul, refreshing for the troubled spirit. A long time later I rose on one elbow and blew out the lamp. My prayer had come through listening, not speaking. Soon I was asleep.

The next morning the yard showed evidence of the night's windstorm. Branches and leaves were everywhere. But the birds were high in the trees, singing, and a saucy blue jay was perched on a branch outside the window, daring me to come outside.

Few people have a place like this where they can go and feel themselves close to the earth. We've become accustomed to asphalt and concrete, exhaust fumes and street lights, the roar of motors and false entertainment of electronic devices. This kind of place would drive most urbanites to madness. But that's because we do not know how to listen—and look. No matter where we are, if we stop and observe, we'll see the face of God in His creation.

36. Sweaty Saints

One of the problems with urban living is we live so close we never get to know each other.

For years I had a next-door neighbor who lived in an entirely different world from me. Our daughter fed their fish when they went off for weekends. I spoke to him when I went out in the morning to pick up the paper from the driveway. I wisecracked at him when I saw him starting his lawnmower. I shouted greetings when we charcoaled in the backyard. I even took his son with us to Sunday school. But I never knew him—even though our bedrooms were less than thirty-five feet apart.

Urban living does that.

A few decades ago your nearest neighbor might be fifteen miles away, but when you saw him at church, the market or the monthly grange meeting, the fellowship was real. If there was a new baby, or sickness, the "neighbors" came to help—and stayed as long as needed. If a new family joined the church, they could expect a housewarming. The pantry would be stocked with good things, the women would hang drapes while the men chopped wood or mowed the pasture. If a family needed a new barn, forty men might show up on a Saturday to "raise the roof." The lady folks would fix a huge dinner and after the work was done, everybody would join in a big square dance in the new barn.

But we don't live like that any more. At least most of us subdivision, apartment and condo dwellers don't. Even those of us who live in "the country" have become isolationists. Too often country living is simply an escape from the mad dash to the office. We still don't have time for neighbors.

If you have a flat tire in your driveway you have to call the service station, because your next-door neighbor will drive right by you. And who among us has not felt the frustration and guilt of seeing an ambulance—or hearse—pull away from a house down the street and realize it is too late to become neighbors. We're just strangers who live close together. We may sit on the same pew but we have no idea where the other person hurts.

If you build a new church building you have to hire it done. How many churches, in this urban age of specialties, busyness and fast living, are built by doctors, lawyers, bankers and engineers who take off early from their jobs to spread tar, tack carpet or varnish pews? Since we're more concerned with the end than the means, we hire it done. As a result we pass up one of the best ways to get close. Sweating together is the beginning of brotherhood.

Recently I got involved in something which—at least in our church in Florida—could reverse this trend. A retired medical missionary, eighty-six-year-old Dr. Nell Holman, had given our church seven acres of land to be developed as a retreat center. For years I've entertained a vision for such a place where foreign missionaries, weary from their overseas ministry, or preparing to leave for the field, could come under the ministry of a loving, caring church for as long as necessary. Cottages would be built, perhaps by other Christians across the nation who would catch the vision, and we could minister to the needs of these missionaries, along with their families, as they had ministered overseas.

Now the land was ours. But there were problems. Most of the property was covered with lush, thick, tropical growth—bamboo, scrub oaks, palm trees, thorn bushes, vines and high grass. Before we could even find the property lines—much less build—we had to clear that jungle.

"Let's hire it done," one man suggested. But another. with deeper insight, thought God might have something more in mind than building a retreat center. Maybe he wanted to build a church—a real church made up of people in relationship.

A simple plea went out Sunday morning. We needed men to clear the land. Early the following Saturday morning sixty men showed up with chain saws, rakes, axes, shovels and machetes. The women came too, some to chop, some to cook. We worked hard in the broiling sun—cutting, clearing, tearing down rotting buildings and burning rubbish in a huge bonfire. At sundown the land was cleared and there were a lot of tired bodies. But something else had happened. The men and women who did not mingle previously, although they had sat near each other in church, now were a fellowship. A sweaty, dirty, laughing, hugging fellowship: the Brotherhood of Blistered Hands.

Sharing a pew—or a driveway—does not make us neighbors. It takes sweat, and sometimes tears. And one of the quickest ways to bring it to pass is to put two strangers on opposite ends of a crosscut saw.

By the way, if your church doesn't have the blister burden—come on down to Florida. Next week we're scheduled to clean out a couple of septic tanks.

37. For God's Sake, Man, Talk to Me!

Last Saturday morning we had a late breakfast. The children had scattered as they often do on a day off from school and I propped up in bed with a manuscript which needed final editing. Mid-morning, after cleaning up the bathroom, making the beds, and running the vacuum, Jackie went down and fixed eggs with cheddar cheese (my favorite), sausage, and grits. I put on a bathrobe and took my work down to the table.

I've been doing this for years—reading while I eat. It saves a great deal of time. In fact, I read while I do a lot of things. I'm perplexed at women who don't seem to have the same sense of efficiency, but then, most women are not given to this masculine type of logical thinking. While a man thinks "One, two, three, four," a woman often thinks, "Nine, thirteen, six, one, forty-two." Or, as someone else said: "A man thinks with his head, a woman with her heart."

Therefore it wasn't unusual for Jackie to eat her

breakfast in silence as I read. Nor was it out of the ordinary for her to finally begin a conversation with the top of my head, which was bent over the well-marked paper beside my now empty plate.

Sipping a cup of spiced tea, she began to ramble about something she had discovered while reading the creation story in Genesis. I grunted an occasional noise of recognition, not really hearing but not wanting to offend her, either.

Like most husbands, I've learned it's best to give an impression of interest. Perhaps it's a hangover from the time I used to rush back to the door of the church after a Sunday morning service to shake hands with my parishioners. Smiling, always smiling. And agreeing. But never really listening. If someone did try to tell me something, I would give him a big "God bless you, brother," all the while pulling him through the door as I shook his hand. This way, to carry on a conversation he'd have to look back over his shoulder, which was discouraging since by that time I'd be shaking hands with the person behind him. It's a trick used by politicians and preachers—both notorious as types of people who never listen.

"Guess what I discovered in Genesis this morning," Jackie said to the top of my head.

"Uh, that's nice," I mumbled, trying not to lose my place. Then vaguely realizing I had given a stupid reply, I added, "Ah . . . what did you learn?"

"I learned that God gave Adam the command not to eat of the tree in the garden long before Eve was created."

"That's interesting," I answered. (By the way, this is a phrase I picked up from Pat Robertson which means, "I don't know what you're talking about, but I don't want to question you since it might stimulate you to keep on talking.")

She kept on talking. "The whole problem with the human race, all the problems of the world, stem from one thing."

She was determined to press on.

"Uh huh, what's that?"

"Adam didn't talk to his wife. That's where all the problems came from. He knew everything God wanted, but he just didn't communicate with Eve. He was too busy 'dressing the garden.' When he wouldn't talk to her, she finally wandered off and found a slick fellow who would talk."

Somehow, in my state of semi-concentration, I sensed I shouldn't pursue this topic of conversation. I adjusted my glasses and hastily blue-penciled a redundant sentence which was trying to creep into print.

"What do you think about that?" Jackie was determined to get some kind of response.

"That's interesting," I mumbled. I could tell by the way the table was vibrating she was about to erupt. Avoiding her eyes, I glanced at my watch, picked up the stack of papers and started out of the room. "Thanks for a great breakfast," I said sincerely. "It's nice to be here with you on Saturday morning."

"But you aren't 'with me,' " she said, a trace of pain in her voice. "All those women out there think you're God's man of faith and power—writing all those things about husbands loving their wives, about men being the priests in their homes, about proper spiritual covering. But all I ever see is the top of your head at the table and the back of your head at the typewriter."

I smiled and patted her shoulder. We make a great team. She makes all the minor decisions such as which college the kids will attend and what brand of tires to put on the car, while I make the big decisions such as how to settle all the problems in the Kingdom. I started up the steps toward my studio, reading as I went. I read while I do a lot of things.

"Where are you going?"

"Well . . . uh . . . er . . . I've got to dress the garden . . . I mean, finish typing this manuscript. By the way, what's for lunch?"

"Apples," she said with a note of resignation. "Fresh from the tree."

I nodded. "Uh . . . that's interesting."

38. The Wonder of It All

Gypsy Smith, a great evangelist from another era, sang and preached his way around the world. He was simple, original, and colorful. He used to say, "I was born in a field; don't try to put me in a flowerpot." And nobody ever did.

Somebody wanted to teach him music and told him he ought to sing from his diaphragm. He snorted and said, "I don't want to sing from my diaphragm. I want to sing from my heart." And he did, right up until he was eighty-seven years of age when he died preaching.

Someone once asked Gypsy what was the secret of the freshness of his ministry. The old man paused, and then with a sparkle that came from the heart, said, "The secret of my ministry is that I've never lost the wonder."

Whether the Gypsy realized it or not, that's the secret to all freshness. Jesus flattened the theologians of His day by saying that only a little child could enter the Kingdom of Heaven.

THE LAST WORD

You see, children haven't lost the sense of wonder. They haven't been here long enough to get used to it all. Anything can happen to a child. Everything is new. Around every corner waits a brand-new surprise, because they've never been there before.

Children, like bears, go over the mountain to see what they can see. Adults go over the mountain in order to buy a twelve-hundred-acre plot of ground and subdivide it into shopping centers.

Only children believe in tooth fairies and lollypops, merry-go-rounds and butterflies, fireflies on a summer night, and fiddler crabs on the beach. Adults never pause and watch the particles of dust swirl in a sunbeam, or put their noses to the ground to watch an ant carry a beetle ten times its size. Adults see clouds as a threat to an afternoon on the golf course, while children look into the sky and see dragons and castles, humpbacked giants and alligators, or flying cows with overshoes. The life of a child is the most exciting, adventurous, and fresh life in the world. All because a child hasn't lost the wonder of it all.

When I was a boy, growing up in what was then the "country," we had time to be still. There was time for a walk in the grove to watch the spiders build their webs, time to sit on the old swinging bridge across the main canal, throw acorns in the water and wonder where the ripples went after they hit the bank. I had time to think. And pray. And do a lot of reflecting on who I was, who God was, and what kind of man I was supposed to be when I grew up.

Now everything is organized, supervised, planned, and programmed. You don't take a walk today, you take an organized hike. Television, computers, and machines do our thinking for us—and our nation falls apart from the top and the bottom with crime in the streets and in the White House.

I can't solve the problems of the world, and very frankly, I doubt if I can have much influence on Washington. But I can do something about myself. And even though I've passed forty and am cresting the hill, I'm determined to regain the wonder. If it means becoming as a little child again, then so be it. After all, there's nothing wrong with flying cows with overshoes.

39. Indestructible

It is a seventy-five-minute ride on the hydrofoil from Hong Kong, across the entrance of the Canton Harbor on the South China Sea, to the Portuguese province of Macao. The tiny, isolated province on the China mainland is a mixture of Eurasians and refugee Chinese. It is separated from Red China by a "no-man's-land" guarded by pillboxes and manned on the Chinese side by soldiers with machine guns. Although many Chinese refugees are able to sneak across the border, there are almost daily reports of guards catching and shooting families who try to escape from the Communist nation.

The week before I arrived, a Chinese woman was machine-gunned to death at the gate of the city. She was one of those with a free passport. That is, she was allowed to pass back and forth from China to Macao. She had been carrying a small baby on her back, but an observant Chinese guard noticed that the baby, which was strapped tightly to the young mother's

133

lower back, had a strange color. When he touched the baby he discovered it was dead. Not only was it dead, but the mother was using the corpse to smuggle jade into Macao. The baby's body had been cut open and was filled with the beautiful green stones which bring a high price in the free city. A quick trial was held outside the guardhouse and within ten minutes the guard captain raised his Tommy gun and executed the young woman on the spot.

Human life is cheap in Asia.

I had a specific purpose in wanting to visit the picturesque city of Macao. Located on the tiny peninsula which is three miles long and one mile wide, the bustling town is a mixture of European and Oriental houses. The "Water People," those refugees who have managed to swim or sneak out of China, live in miserable poverty along the harbor. Up on the hillside are the wealthy homes of retired Europeans. But overlooking the entire peninsula are the remains of the old St. Paul's Cathedral. It was to visit St. Paul's that I came to Macao.

The huge cathedral was built by the Jesuits in 1604. It stood for more than a hundred years before a giant typhoon proved stronger than the work of man's hands. The building fell in ruins, leaving standing only the massive front wall which overlooks the entrance to the harbor. High on the weatherbeaten, jutting wall, challenging the elements down through the years, stands a great bronze cross. It was that cross I came to see.

In 1825 Sir John Bowering sailed his ship into the harbor at Macao and caught a glimpse of that indestructible cross. For more than an hour he stood at the rail of his rocking ship, staring at the free-standing cross with tear-filled eyes. His own personal world was falling apart. His wife was dying. His career fading. He turned from the cross and walked down the narrow steps to his cabin. There he picked up a quill and wrote words which are still familiar to many of us.

Indestructible

In the cross of Christ I glory,
Towering o'er the wrecks of time;
All the light of sacred story
Gathers round its head sublime.

John Bowering was right, I concluded, as I boarded the powerful hydrofoil to return to Hong Kong. Human life is cheap. Mothers kill their babies to smuggle jade. Communists shoot young women without the faintest trace of mercy or sadness. People live in wretched poverty and disease. Yet despite all man's attempts to destroy God—and each other—the cross of Christ still stands . . . o'er the wrecks of time.

40. Listen to the Quiet

Henry Ford once said he didn't want executives who had to work all the time. He insisted that the man who was always in the fevered flurry of activity was not doing his best work. He added that he wanted his executives to clear off their desks, prop their feet on them, and dream some fresh dreams.

His philosophy was only he who has the luxury of time can originate a creative thought.

An American writer, Bill Emmerson, once said: "Time is too precious to crowd." This is an axiom. To be creative one has to deal directly with the problem, then retreat from it long enough to allow the yeasting of the mind to operate. In a quiet mood it breaks forth in splendor from its imprisonment.

Great thinkers—those who create worthwhile ideas—are men who take time. Thoreau wandered through the woods of New England, or spent time sitting on the bank of Walden Pond. But that's the difference between spending time—and being

137

wasted by it.

You don't kill time, you know. It kills you—by forcing you to do things you don't want to do.

The Apostle Paul knew nothing of the speeding luxuries of automobiles and jet planes. He took long walks down dusty paths—sometimes walking as much as a hundred miles at a time. He went sailing. When he was shipwrecked he saw it as an opportunity to create with his mind rather than as a delay in his schedule. (After all, he was on his way to his own execution.) And his times in prison, without benefit of watch or calendar, were used to bless the entire world.

Some people are adept at making on-the-spot decisions, but very few can be creative under imposed pressure. Creativity does not come by force-feeding, super-intensity, and lots of motion. Nor is it necessarily brought about by deadlines (Editors, take note!).

I often differentiate between what the world looks upon as the successful man—the go-getter type—and the man of God who goes after nothing, but waits for God to capture him.

Creativity takes time. Occasionally I will find myself stomping around the house complaining about the lack of privacy that every writer needs to accomplish his work. My wife will reply by saying, "Well, you have twenty minutes before you leave for the airport, why not sit down and write." If she only knew that there are times I withdraw into my studio, close the door, and sit for hours without ever touching the keys of my typewriter—just praying, thinking, and waiting for the Holy Spirit to break through my crust with an idea.

One of life's most sure principles is that when you stop smelling the flowers, get out of your hammock and race to a meeting, or rush to catch a departing vehicle—you do the wrong thing. In most cases the celebration of life means being late for something unimportant.

I grew up in a town that had no public clocks. The only signal of time was the blowing of the fire whistle (which was positioned on top of the town water tower) at noon. That meant it was time to go to lunch. Everyone was always late for everything—for each other's sakes. People got up at "dawn"—rather than 6:05 A.M. They went to bed "after sunset." Ask a man when he'd be there and he'd answer "Directly," which in the south does not mean *at once,* rather it means *after a while.* And lunch was eaten when the fire whistle announced it was noon. Yankees called us "lazy." But we only had one town doctor and didn't need him very much. Nobody ever got divorced. And a lot of people had time to write, paint, and love.

When I forget what time it is, I always discover I have better moments. I still remember my first camping trip into the Sinai. We were to be gone for ten days, taking a four-wheel-drive vehicle into the heart of the desert and then hiking and climbing mountains. Our guide insisted we leave our watches at the hotel in Jerusalem. "If you want to hear God as Moses did," she said seriously, "you have to leave your watches behind." For three days I felt naked. Then I felt free.

The ideas that make most people famous are not original. The truth or insight really breaks upon them from the outside. (Even this concept was stimulated by a thought from Henry Ford.) The pressure of time is the greatest barrier to creativity and originality. God is constantly desiring to pour His truth into us—but if we are busy moving it is often like trying to pour milk into your child's glass, when he has that glass in his hand and is sneezing at the same time.

Yet once the idea takes hold, it sets up chain reactions which become original until the creative person is almost seized by the entire concept. No longer does the idea belong to Henry Ford. Now it is mine. And when you finish reading this—it will be yours.

Maybe we should listen to the wisdom of quietness if we are pressed by crowded social calendars, impossible timetables, overburdened appointment books or mountains of correspondence on our desks.

Yet, to find a place to be alone on this crowded planet is almost impossible. Cocktail parties may help a person kill time (that is, if time is so meaningless that you live your life in boredom), but crowded rooms seldom spawn great flashes of inspiration. There is too much small talk, idle chatter, and wasted words. Insight and inspiration usually come in the alone hours, after cleansing our minds through prayer and refilling them with the Word of God. There, sans telephones and chattering friends, God can speak.

For a number of years I wanted a room in our house where I could go alone to pray. A room devoid of desk, kitchen cabinets, or telephone. Then we bought a large house in the country and discovered the former owner had built a "happy hour room" next to the den. We took out the bar, installed an altar, and turned it into a chapel and prayer room. Some of my greatest moments of insight into my own personal problems, or the problems faced by my friends and family, come when I enter this small, wood-paneled room, shut the doors and kneel at the little altar. I'm sure the former owner would shake his head in dismay, but I don't think he knew how close to the truth he was when he called it a "happy hour room."

It is reported that St. Francis said these words: "Human nature is like a pool of water, my Lord. Cast a stone therein, it goes rough and broken; stir it, it becomes foul; give it peace, let it rest, and it will reflect the face of the heavens which lie over it."

41. All God's Chillun Got Shoes

It wasn't too many years ago that any man who appeared in public wearing patent leather shoes was suspect. I mean, it wasn't safe to sit beside him in the bus station. But times changed. And the day arrived when I finally consented to join the gang and buy a pair of shiny, black patent leather loafers.

For two years Jackie nagged me about my old, scuffed, mail-order shoes. "It's bad enough that you insist on wearing tennis shoes to church here at home," she complained. "But I'm ashamed to travel with you out of town. You always wear those six-year-old $7.95 specials made out of plastic. If Bob Mumford can wear patent leather shoes, you can too. You need to present a better image."

It's not that I objected to a better image. It's just that new shoes always pinched my feet. Besides, it was hard for me to believe that shiny shoes would make me look more masculine.

Then a friend of mine, who ran a shoe store in Vero Beach,

made the kind of offer I couldn't refuse. "If you'll throw away those old clodhoppers," he said after attending church services one Sunday in Melbourne, "I'll give you a new pair of shoes." Since the one thing I hated more than wearing new shoes was shopping for them, I let Jackie go pick them out. Now that was something else I'd never done before. But then, I'd never worn shiny shoes before either.

The next day we were to leave for an important conference in North Carolina. Jackie put her foot down when I tried to pack my tennis shoes. "Furthermore," she insisted, "I want you to wear your new shoes on the plane."

It was my first time to try them on. Even though they were the correct size, they gripped my feet like vises. "They loosen up as you wear them," Jackie assured me as I hobbled from the departure lounge to the plane.

By the time we reached Atlanta, however, the pain was excruciating. We had to change planes and I limped into the terminal. While Jackie made a quick phone call back home, I collapsed into a chair. Anger, like molten lava, was boiling inside me. How could I possibly preach that night with my feet hurting so? If I only had brought my comfortable old shoes. No, I had to be a Mr. Milquetoast, pushed around by my wife. A guy walked by. He was wearing tennis shoes—and whistling. It was more than I could stand. It was all Jackie's fault, her and her desire to improve my image and to make me wear Mumford shoes. Well, image be hanged if it caused my feet to suffer untold agony.

By the time Jackie returned I was ready to explode. Before I could say a word, however, she pointed at my foot. "What's that piece of paper sticking out of your shoe?"

I had a sinking feeling in the pit of my stomach. I quickly put my hand over the area and snorted, "It's nothing."

Now she was giggling. "Take your shoes off."

I resisted, but finally pulled them off. To my utter mortification, I found I had failed to remove the cardboard liners. I felt my face turn cherry red as I sheepishly pulled out the thick cardboard and replaced my shoes on my feet. Ah! Comfort! And with it a grateful prayer that God had kept my mouth shut.

The following Sunday I entered church on the arm of my wife—wearing my flashy new patent leather pumps. And surprisingly enough, my only concern was that some tennis-shoe-wearing clod might step on them and leave scratches.

42. Deliver Me from Hell Rocks

Whoever invented hard candy (known through the rest of this chapter as "Hell Rocks") should be forced to sit in a dentist's chair every afternoon from three until five while the mad driller whirrs away without the aid of painkillers.

I used to think the worst thing which could happen to your teeth was a substance known as "Black Cow," a stiff, chewy candy on a stick invented by an unemployed dentist. But Black Cows, although obviously demonic in nature, only pull out fillings and loosen teeth. Hell Rocks break them off.

Teeth, of course, are not like lizard tails that grow back. Once they are gone, they are gone forever. Not only that, teeth protect a tiny nerve that runs from your jaw to your toes. When you break one off you expose this nerve, which then makes all parts of your body suffer as though someone were tugging at your fingernails with a pair of pliers. Therefore, along with heroin and chewing tobacco, Hell Rocks are forbidden in our house.

Then someone, probably the same person who puts razor blades in apples at Hallowe'en, gave our children some Hell Rocks for Christmas. I gave them a long sermon about their dangers, similar to the sermon my mother gave me thirty-five years ago when someone gave me a deck of playing cards. "I'd rather you took a drink of demon rum than chew Hell Rocks," I told them.

After all, demon rum can only lead to a drunkard's grave. Hell Rocks break off your teeth—a fate worse than death.

Somehow, though, in our haste to get packed as we left for a Christmas vacation, the Hell Rocks found their way into the bag of food to be eaten on the train. There they remained, hidden away with Stygian cleverness, until the next morning when the children were all out of the compartment. I happened to be browsing through the brown paper sack when I spotted them, beckoning to me from under the Fig Newtons.

Every spiritual principle in me warned me to have nothing to do with them. "Rebuke them," the voice on my shoulder said. "Flush them. Quickly." But even as Eve fondled the apple, so I played the role of the fool and picked them up, slowly entertaining the malevolent thought that just one couldn't hurt me.

"Ye shall not surely die," the familiar voice said from the other shoulder.

How many times have I faced the arch-fiend? And how many times have I answered that man does not live by bread alone? But surely just a little candy. . . .

Casting a furtive glance over my shoulder to make sure none of the children were coming down the aisle, I plunked a Hell Rock into my mouth. The specter of eating forbidden fruit, of diametrically disobeying what I had commanded my own children not to do, was, for the moment, compensated by the sweet taste. Then I did the unpardonable. I bit down.

Instantly I broke off my next to last molar on the upper left side. I could feel the cool air hit the exposed nerve, sending shivers all the way to my toes. Then the piece of tooth was floating around in my mouth and I could feel the jagged edge of what was left with the edge of my tongue. I looked for my tempter to rebuke him, but he was gone—leaving behind only the echo of his haunting laugh. Another saint had gone down in defeat.

A week and two days later—after a week and two days of agony—sitting in a dentist's chair from three until five while the mad driller whirred away, I developed a strong sympathy for Adam and Eve as they left the garden. Some place behind the dentist's chair I sensed the presence of an angel with flaming sword, reminding me I could never, never return to the world of chewing hard things—even to the pleasure of chewing up ice.

Sin has a way of finding you out. But Hell Rocks, unlike Longfellow's mills, do not grind slowly. They get things done in a hurry.

43. I Don't Throw Things Like I Used To

We've just had to replace the windshield in our Chevrolet station wagon. Our teenage son, Tim, who had an argument with his girlfriend, lost his temper. In a fit of frustration he slammed his hand against the windshield—cracking the glass.

I'm not sure how our insurance company is going to respond to my claim. But I know how my wife responded.

"Like father, like son!"

She's right. But she's wrong, too. There was a long period in my life when I vented most of my frustrations with fits of rage and anger. She was witness to most of these—in some cases, even the victim.

It goes back a long way. Jackie was there that night in the Orange Bowl stadium, back in 1949, when I was playing defensive tackle and we were trailing better than 40-0. Now that can be pretty frustrating. The opposing team had put in their third team and they were still scoring with ease. When the fat guard in front of me, who had just come off the bench for the first time all year, squatted down in position and spit on me through his nose guard, it was the end of the day for me. I busted my fist against the side of his helmet and tried to claw my way through his shoulder pads to get a piece of meat. Of course I was tossed out of the game, but my presence didn't seem to be making a great deal of difference in the score anyway.

In the early years of our marriage I sometimes treated her the same way. The slightest provocation would send me off into a maniacal frenzy, slamming doors, kicking walls, poking my fist through closet doors, and on several occasions hurling dishes—sometimes full of things like string beans or coleslaw—across the kitchen to smash them against walls or floor. Only the grace of God kept me from falling into the category of a "wife-beater"; only God, and Jackie, both knew I was capable of it.

Then something happened. I was thirty-six years old when the Holy Spirit invaded those secret areas of my life and began to bring conformity to the image of Christ. It wasn't an overnight thing—this experience. Oh, the baptism in the Holy Spirit was an experience, but the subsequent "filling" of the Holy Spirit is still taking place. That means there are still areas yet untouched; or if touched, not yet saturated.

I still break a few things, bend a few things, and occasionally even throw something. But the episodes are growing less frequent—and the times of forgiveness more precious.

I have known for a long time the Bible taught I should be "slow to anger." But it also teaches I should love my neighbor and a lot of other impossible commands. Self-control, like the other fruit of the spirit, always seems to dangle just out of my reach But in the "infilling" of the Holy Spirit, I am gradually realizing the possibility of receiving the character of Jesus. I've not arrived—but things sure are better.

Now, it seems, I have an obligation to pass that possibility along to the other knuckle-cracker in the family, my teenage son. Since his experience with the windshield he's been a lot more willing to learn. A bruised hand and loss of allowance have a way of doing strange things—even opening our ears so we can hear God. And, in this case, to hear him through an old pro who has been there before.

44. Never Obsolete

In a society where old age is looked upon as a curse, and rebellion among children as a virtue, the command to "honor thy father and mother" sounds strange, almost antiquated. Yet like all absolutes, it remains despite the changing times.

A year ago, when my brothers and sister began to think about plans for our parents' golden wedding anniversary, it seemed simply a nice thing to do. I mean, after all, it's hard enough to remain married for five years these days. How many stick it out for fifty? However, as the time grew nearer, it became evident we were doing more than celebrating fifty years of marriage. This was an opportunity to actually put the biblical command into practice—to pay homage to our father and mother.

We did that last Sunday afternoon. It wasn't an elaborate occasion. Friends did most of the work—preparing a reception, fixing food, decorating the place where we met. All the children did was show up.

THE LAST WORD

It was my older brother, Clay, who set the theme for the gathering. "There is only one 'command with promise,' " Clay, an army major general, said. "God commands us to honor our father and mother. In turn, He promises us long life. But even if the reward were not there, I would still obey the order of the Commanding General." It took a lot of red tape cutting, but Clay flew in from his command post in Germany to obey the higher command.

My younger brother, John, left his busy medical practice to drive across the state. My sister flew in from Missouri.

All, by common consent, realized this should take priority over any other function. Honor thy father and mother does not grow obsolete just because parents grow old. If anything, it grows more absolute. It is not an option—it is a command.

Saturday night, after we had returned from an intimate meal, the family gathered in the front room of the house for a time of reminiscing. Each child has gained a measure of independent fame and success. But sitting together on the eve of the anniversary, we were not generals or doctors or writers—we were children, eager to soak from our parents all the wisdom they were willing to share.

With a little coaxing, we were able to get daddy on his feet for a speech. Instead of a speech, however, he gave us a legacy. "What is most important?" he asked. He answered the question by paraphrasing Daniel Webster. "My relationship with God is most important." Then he listed, in descending order, the other things that were most important in his life—his wife, children, grandchildren, and friends.

"What would I do for a friend?" he asked. "Everything," he answered. "And my friends have demonstrated that they would do as much for us. What a wonderful world is our world among friends."

I thought about all this the next afternoon. The gala reception was over. The family returned to the house and gathered around the piano as we used to do. Clay was at the keyboard. Dr. John pitched his tenor voice against my baritone and sister Audrey joined in with an alto. We sang the old time songs: "The Man On the Flying Trapeze," "Silver Threads Among the Gold." Then we heard daddy's bass voice joining in and mother's soprano. We were a family again . . . and always will be, because we have honored father and mother.

45. Looking Down the Road to the Opera House

At age thirty-nine, my wife started taking piano lessons. Up until three weeks before she had never put her fingers on the keyboard of our piano except to dust it off with an old rag which smelled of furniture polish. But something happened. Perhaps it was the realization that she was about to pass the crest of her life without ever having the thrill of doing the unordinary—dreaming the impossible dream. Maybe it was the fact she lived with a husband who was always taking off to some exotic place and leaving her behind because she couldn't stand the bugs—or the lack of sanitary facilities. Whatever the motivation, one morning I came downstairs and she was sitting awkwardly on the piano bench, a big red and white Thompson book propped in front of her, playing with one finger a vulgarized rendition of "The Volga Boatman."

I stood on the bottom step listening. It was the same song I had begun with thirty years before—in my first piano lesson.

157

"Dee, dee, daa, DUHM. Dee, dee, daa, DUHM. Dee, daa, dee, doo; Dee, dee, daa, DUHM."

My mind ran back to Miss Rebecca Rodenberg, a sweet-faced second grade teacher, who also taught piano in the upstairs room of the First Methodist Church. There I sat at a battered old upright, picking out "Dee, dee, daa, DUHM," and experiencing the thrill of holding the pedal down all the way through "The Bells of St. Mary's."

Actually Jackie was far ahead of where I started. Miss Rodenberg not only had to teach me music, she had to teach me how to recognize my right hand from my left hand. Up until then there had been no need to make a distinction. But in piano-playing you have to know, for the bottom notes are the lefties and the top ones righties.

Fortunately, Jackie already knew her left hand from her right. But she was having the same problem I had in finding the notes. In my case, middle C was directly under a big keyhole in the old upright. Our piano doesn't have a keyhole, so middle C is two notes down from the note with the chipped ivory.

I hope she sticks it out. I didn't. I took for an additional three years from Mrs. Charles Jewett, but then piano began to get in the way of football and girls. I became a piano dropout. And for the next thirty years my repertoire was limited to things I could play in the key of C—mostly "Silent Night," "The Marine Hymn," and something called "The Happy Farmer."

While in graduate school we bought an old upright clunker and I started taking piano again—this time from a music professor at the seminary. But it was too late. She shook her head, after eight months of trying, and told me I had picked up too many bad habits—primarily that of playing only on the white notes. So I dropped out again and settled for letting my children—and now my wife—pick up where I left off.

In looking back on why I never made it as a piano player I realize it was the same thing which often separates me from being a great writer or a devoted Christian. Discipline, or in my case, lack of it. Discipline, sacrifice and a sense of priorities are the hidden elements which distinguish the great from the mediocre.

I remember, as a college student, attending the Washington Opera House and hearing the master violinist, Fritz Kreisler. As an encore, he put the bow to strings and played "Humoresque" as only he could. As the last notes faded there was not a dry eye among the evening dress crowd. Then, as one, that massive crowd stood to their feet. Not a whisper. Not a sound. Total silence—which is the greatest applause an audience can ever give. From where I was, in the far back, I could see the master musician on stage, his silver hair glittering under the spots, his violin hanging free, tucked between his chin and shoulder, as he stood with bowed head, bow in hand.

I remembered something that night, as we left the opera house. It was something Fritz Kreisler had written many years before. "Narrow is the road that leads to the life of a violinist." But at that moment, standing alone on the stage, having just finished a perfect rendition of a musical masterpiece which touched the hearts of the hundreds present, I had no doubt that he regretted not a moment of the practice and discipline and sacrifice which brought him there.

I left Jackie to her Volga Boatman and went about my business for the morning. I doubted seriously if she would ever make it to the Washington Opera House. In fact, I doubted if she would ever really learn to play the piano. But I admired her for trying, for being willing to dare to do the impossible and pay the price of discipline, even if for only a little while.

46. Now Let's All Impress God

The folks at our little church decided they wanted an altar rail. "That floor is mighty uncomfortable if you stay down very long," one man said. He was referring to kneeling on the old, cracked tile at the front of the room we used for public worship.

"If we just had some place to kneel it would make things easier," another said.

As buildings go, our old "sheepshed" isn't much to look at. We began with an old childcare center. The men knocked out a wall, repainted the woodwork, and scraped up as much of the rotting, broken vinyl tile as they could. They built a pulpit, bought metal chairs and "drug in" an old clunker of a piano with half the ivories missing. What we didn't have was an altar rail.

Someone suggested carpet, but I kept remembering something my daddy said a long time ago. "When a church lays thick carpet, people with dirty shoes aren't welcomed any longer."

So we decided to wait on the carpet until our attitude was right. But in order to get our attitude right, we needed an altar rail. We started looking.

The following week a friend of mine took me on a guided tour of one of the most beautiful church sanctuaries I've ever seen. I had spoken in the social hall and he later grabbed my arm to show off the building. It was late afternoon and the building was empty when we entered the narthex. The afternoon sun was streaming through the beautiful stained glass windows and falling softly across the empty pews. I was awed by its beauty.

As we tiptoed down the aisle, ankle deep in the plush carpet, I noted my friend was glancing at my shoes. I breathed a sigh of relief. No mud there. Not today. He nodded approvingly and pointed out the stained glass windows and told me the price. He gestured toward the organ and told me the price. He pointed out the amplifying system and told me the price.

"Surely even God would be impressed with this," I thought.

In a room behind the nave I spotted the portable altar rail. It was hand carved from solid ash with deep velvet padding. My guide told me, in hushed tones, that it was used during communion services several times a year.

"What would happen if someone came down the aisle one morning," I asked innocently, "and threw himself upon the altar rail and cried out for God to touch his life?"

He looked at me in shock. "You mean people still do things like that? Maybe we shouldn't use the rail at all if it might encourage that kind of action."

"It certainly could happen," I said innocently. "Folks are picking up a lot of strange ideas these days. Maybe you ought to give the altar rail away rather than run the risk."

I felt bad the moment I said it. But, on the other hand, I enjoyed letting the words slip out of my mouth.

"Well, we can't stand a disturbance now," he said seriously. "If you only knew how far in debt we are—paying for this building. . . ."

I started to suggest I knew someone who could use the altar rail. Then I thought of the cracked tile floor, the hard metal chairs, and somehow I just couldn't picture that handcarved, velvet-covered piece of furniture in there.

"Maybe you better keep it," I said. "It just might be that a prophet might decide to visit your church some Sunday. You know they always like to kneel and worship before they stand and prophesy. It would be a shame not to have an altar rail."

He looked at me strangely, blinked rapidly a number of times, then said hurriedly, "Now, let me show you our magnificent rest rooms. . . ."

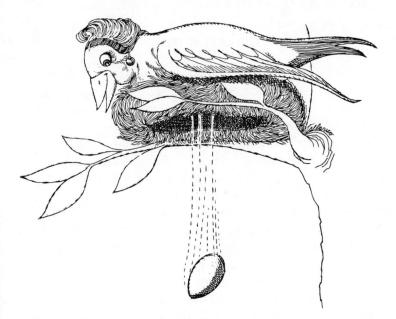

47. Call for Disciples

In my more honest moments I cannot help but question why we do not see more "signs and wonders" in our Christian walk. It is true that accompanying the new move of the Holy Spirit, there are miracles, healings and dramatic answers to prayer. But when I sit back and reflect on the way things really are, I am forced to admit we still fall far short of the standard set by the New Testament church in the Book of Acts. There it seems there were miracles every day. Nothing was impossible—from the healing of mental illness to the raising of the dead. We see almost none of this. Why?

Last year during a windstorm one of the big Australian pines behind our house toppled to the ground. It took three of us working two days to cut it up and haul it away. When I asked a tree expert what had caused the tree to fall he said simply, "It outgrew its root system." In other words, it was too tall for its foundation. When the wind came, over it went.

THE LAST WORD

It seems one of the weaknesses among those desiring to move up to "normal" Christianity—where signs and wonders are a daily occurrence—is the tendency to climb higher before our foundation has been secured.

Jesus said on Judgment Day there will be some to step forward with a long list of accomplishments, including healing the sick and casting out demons. Yet their works will not be acceptable because they only *heard* His commandments, they did not practice them personally.

That's heavy teaching. To explain it, Jesus talked about the necessity of putting down a foundation before building a house. Otherwise the first spring rain will wash you away.

The rock foundation is discipleship. Jesus said His disciples would one day see signs and wonders accompanying their ministry. But the wise man needs to stop and reflect: those words were not given to the multitude, only to a few—and then as a graduation address three years after intensive training in discipleship.

I believe the reason we're not seeing more signs and wonders is we don't have more disciples. We seem to be spawning a generation of people who don't have time to wait on the Lord. People who don't have time to live disciplined lives, pressured always by the need to "get something done for God." All want to see miracles—few are willing to pay the price for them.

In Jesus' brand of discipleship there are prerequisites for maturity. Before healing the sick there is a necessity of being committed to the Great Physician. There is a need for daily repentance. For forgiveness of all who have wronged us. Homes are to be in divine order. Each of us is to be submitted to a local body. The disciplines of giving, fasting, and praying must be established in our personal lives. Only then can we move on to signs and wonders.

One of my favorite stories has to do with a mother bird who built a beautiful nest high in a tree. Only the nest had no bottom. When questioned about it, the mother said, "Oh, I just love to lay eggs but I hate the responsibility of having to raise babies."

Most of us have been caught in the "soul-winners-syndrome." Jesus, however, never commanded His followers to win souls. Rather, He told them to go out and make disciples.

Making disciples means sticking with a person long after he has entered the Kingdom. Riding herd over him, much as a cowboy watches the dogies—the motherless calves—or as a shepherd watches the lambs. It means seeing people through. It means sticking with a person for years, if necessary, until he comes into full maturity. It means seeing the potential of a Simon Peter when, even after three years of intense training, he lets you down.

We brag about winning thousands. Jesus was satisfied with eleven.

I remember talking with a Christian professor on the campus of a large university in Brno, Czechoslovakia. "Our small group has set a goal for those who will come into the Kingdom next year," he said.

I vividly remembered the goals my own denomination had set back in the States. A million more in Fifty-Four. Thirty thousand new churches next year. "What's your goal?" I asked.

"Three!" he said with determination. "We are claiming three Communists for Jesus next year." Then he added with excitement, "And one of them has already accepted Christ. Unfortunately, he was immediately imprisoned, but we're still nourishing him along in the Lord."

Christianity is more than obstetrics. It is pediatrics, public health, internal medicine, diagnostic care, surgery, and finally geriatrics. In short, it is a life of discipleship. Years after Jesus returned to heaven, His followers were still known as His disciples. You never outgrow it.

THE LAST WORD

Shortly after graduating from the seminary I was called as the associate pastor in a large southern church. My task was to serve the senior pastor who had been there almost twenty years and was about ready to retire. Shortly after I arrived the senior pastor had a serious heart attack. The deacons waited until he was well enough to come back to work—and then fired him. Just a year before he was eligible to retire.

The shock of seeing church leaders treat their shepherd in such an inhuman way made a lasting scar on my spirit. Even more vivid, however, was sitting with the old pastor as he cleared out his desk, packing things away in a suitcase in preparation for moving into a small apartment and trying to find a job.

"If I had it to do all over again," he said sadly, reflecting on his more than forty years in the ministry, "I would not concentrate on the masses. I would spend my life with ten men, teaching them to be like Jesus. These men who fired me are all active soul-winners. I trained them to be that way. But I failed to instill in them the character of the Master. And now I am paying the price."

My prayer for the Body of Christ is not that there should be more miracle ministries. Rather, I would hear the commendation of the Master for our maturity in discipleship.

48. *Glimpsing the Edge of Eternity*

It snowed the day we arrived in Franklin, North Carolina, and the mountains were covered with a soft, white blanket of freshness. I stood in front of the little cabin and watched it float down, gently, silently, appearing out of the dark sky and forming soft, fluorescent circles around the yellow porch lights. I stood there for a long time, watching the snow drift down, clinging to the bare twigs of the elm trees, settling on the tops of the boxwoods near the stone foundation, brushing against my ears and eyelashes, covering the earth with a soft blanket of peace.

The mountain cottage at the end of the winding dirt road belonged to George Sowerby, a minister friend of mine. Designed to accommodate eight persons, that night there were thirty-seven of us crowded around the roaring fireplace—most of them young people from George's church in Fort Pierce, Florida.

169

THE LAST WORD

We sat in a circle in front of the fire. Through the picture window we could see the big snowflakes drifting silently through the night. Inside the crackling fire accompanied us while we sang nonsense songs and spirituals, followed by a time of discussion and prayer.

After the kids were bedded down, the girls on the floor and the boys in sleeping bags in a camper trailer, I walked up the dark, snow-covered road toward Cowee Bald. The sky had cleared, revealing a billion stars twinkling in the clear, cold night. The only sound was the gurgling of a small mountain stream beside the road and the soft crunch of my shoes in the snow. All the other night noises were smothered, leaving me with the impression of standing alone on earth.

I wondered about the time, but to glance at my watch would have been sacrilegious. Clocks, calendars, automobiles, and airplanes—instruments of time and speed—were all buried beneath nature's cloak of stillness and slowness. I kicked the snow with my boot, and standing in the middle of the road, threw my head back and breathed deeply of the pine-scented air. Looking into the heavens I could see stars whose light had left there a million years ago, and realized I was just glimpsing the edge of space. Beyond that was infinity—and surrounding it all, the Creator.

I remembered a quote from the German philosopher, Kant. Something about two irrefutable evidences of the existence of God: the moral law within and the starry universe above. I breathed His name: "God."

Then, overwhelmed by His presence, I called Him what I had learned to call Him through experience: "Father!"

The next morning the sun had come out, transforming the countryside into a veritable fairyland of brilliance. Every branch had its own overcoat, every twig its own diamond. I had just returned from a walk up the mountain to the waterfall which cascaded down icicle-shrouded boulders. I dreaded catching the jet to New York that afternoon, preferring to stay isolated where I was.

But I have stories to tell. George has sermons to preach. The young people have a witness to bear. None of us can remain in isolation—even with God. For even Jesus told His disciples they could not remain on the mountain top with Him—there was too much to do in the valley. So I turned my back and headed out. Thankful that for two days my world had slowed to a stop beneath a blanket of winter innocence, and I was a better man because of it.

49. I Wish You Wouldn't Look in My Closet

I'm having a hard time enjoying my Filipino houseguest. Already his presence has upset my way of living—a way in which I have grown very comfortable. The alternatives are not pleasant; either get rid of him or change my way of living.

I first met Aley Gonzalez three years before my first visit to the southernmost island of the archipelago: Mindanao. An ex-boxer with more than a hundred professional fights under his bantam-weight belt, this middle-aged, tough-as-coconut-husk, brown-skinned Filipino was preaching like he fought in the ring—both hands jabbing, feet dancing and always boring in for the knockout punch. With the aid of a vintage motorcycle and motorized outrigger canoe, he would go into some of the most inaccessible places in the island chain, starting churches and training pastors.

His average salary was fifty pesos a month (about seven dollars) and his entire wardrobe consisted of three pair of pants, some shirts, a cheap nylon jacket and a pair of rubber slaps.

Few Americans ever visit his out-of-the-way location in the province of Agusan del Norte. To get there you go seven hundred miles south from Manila, cross two volcanos, through the straits at Mactan, take a jeep ride through the rain forests to the coastal barrio of Cabadbaran. Those of us who had visited there, however, had encouraged Aley to visit the States. It would surely broaden his perspective and make him a better preacher. Or, so we thought.

Then Aley arrived at my Florida home. My son Tim had worked that summer and saved money for an expensive new slalom water ski. Knowing how much Aley loved the water (we had spent some happy hours swimming together in the China Sea) I took him with us for a late afternoon ride in our new boat.

On the way to the marina we passed a golf course.

"Why do those men hit that little ball with those sticks?" he asked. "Does somebody hire them to do that?"

I started to give him an explanation but realized it sounded foolish, so I stopped. "We have a lot of people in America who do odd things," I mumbled.

Aley nodded. He understood.

"We hear in the Philippines there are many Americans without work. When jobs become more plentiful they will probably stop this foolishness."

I didn't have the heart to tell him that only the rich could afford to be fools.

Aley was impressed with my boat.

"It is very expensive," he said softly, running his hands along the sleek fiberglass deck. "It must have cost twenty thousand pesos. But what do you use it for? Do your sons and daughters fish for a living?"

He could tell I was having trouble with an answer.

"Perhaps you and your wife go up and down the river and preach the Gospel to all those out-of-work people swinging their sticks at the balls?" he asked, knowing that somewhere I had hidden a sensible answer.

When I explained we used the boat only to pull water skiers and for some sport fishing, he was startled. I could tell he was thinking of the thirty-two miles he had to paddle his outrigger just to get to the small village of San Jose where he preached the Gospel. And here I was with this sleek red-and-white fiberglass beauty. He turned his eyes away and said nothing.

Coming back we stopped at the home of a friend who has three motorcycles in the garage. Aley's eyes danced with excitement, thinking of his battered old Kawasaki.

"These people must go many places helping the poor, feeding the hungry and preaching the Gospel," he said approvingly.

When I explained that although these people belonged to the church they weren't active Christians, he was startled. "You have church members who do not preach? How can this be? The Bible says all church members should be preaching the Gospel. What then do they use these motorcycles for?"

I explained they were dirt bikes, used only to roar around the woods, going no place. I saw that same pensive look move across his face like clouds over the sun. "There are many things about America which I need to learn," he said, amazed.

I drove home a different way. I didn't want him to see the yachts on the river, the dune buggies in the driveways, or the imposing church buildings which sit idle except for a few feeble groans on Sunday morning. I didn't want to face any more of his questions. It was the same feeling I had many years ago when, as a young idealist, I attended a church service when they dedicated a seventy-five-thousand-dollar stained-glass window—to the glory of God.

But I have mellowed since then. (A state which I imagine Aley would describe as one step removed from going rotten.)

Aley was too kind to say anything to me. But last night I

couldn't help but see the expression on his face when he looked in my closet and saw all those shoes.

I haven't been sleeping well recently.

50. Is the Bucket Half Full— or Half Empty?

When you have a family of five children—all in the teenage range—you seldom get the whole gang together. But on a Monday night, after the Sunday services, it was necessary to call a conference at the dining table.

The topic of discussion was a problem which had arisen at the church service the night before. Three-fourths of the way through the service a gang of teenagers got up and walked out. They were led by my oldest son, Bruce.

I hadn't noticed since I was intent on listening to the sermon. But other folks noticed it. A great many of them. Afterwards they quickly informed me that it was my bushy-headed boy who led the pack. "And you're supposed to be the spiritual leader of this flock," one lady pertly reminded me.

Such reminders are always nice to have—especially when they are given in love. So I decided on the family conference.

I refrained from mentioning it until we had finished dessert at the table. Then I said as sternly as possible, "We have a serious matter to discuss. I'm calling us into a business meeting."

"Yes sir, sarge," my youngest daughter, Sandy, said as she stood up at her chair and gave me a crooked salute.

"Stupid," Tim said, glaring at her. "You don't salute sarges. They salute you. Dad's a general, not a sergeant."

"Now this is serious business," I said. "Cut out the horseplay. Bruce walked out of church last night and I want to know why."

Robin, just a year or so younger than Bruce, giggled through her hand. "I knew you'd get caught," she said.

Bruce sat with his head down and bottom lip poked out. Our middle girl, Bonnie, snickered. "We told him not to, but he did it anyway."

Bruce glowered across the table at his two sisters. "Well, you walked out, too."

"Oh, I didn't know that," I said, looking at the two older girls who had now turned a brilliant red. "What I thought was a simple protest now sounds like a mutiny. However, I still hold Bruce responsible because he's the oldest and he led the way."

"But the service was too long," Bruce mumbled into his plate.

"I know," I sighed. "But that's no reason to walk out."

Suddenly, my patient, gentle son turned on me with fury in his voice. "Why is it you always pick on us?" he shouted. "You never tell us we do anything right. All you do is tell us what we do wrong. At least we were in church and not out smoking pot like a lot of other kids."

I was stunned. Not at his violent, rebellious answer, but at the rightness of what he said. Now it was my time to hang my head and look at my plate. When was the last time I had commended them for doing right? I couldn't remember.

Sensing he had stung me, he apologized. "I'm sorry, dad, but all you do is point out our mistakes."

"No, don't back up, Bruce," I said. "You're right this time.

I'm going to have to put you all on restriction for last night's bad show. But I'm going on restriction with you—for copping out as a daddy."

That night I did something which I should have been doing all along—something which I have continued to do every night I have been home from that time on. I made the rounds at bedtime and sat on the side of each bed, praying with each child. Equally important, I spent a few minutes majoring on the things that were right in each life, the things I was genuinely proud of. It seemed important to close the day with words of encouragement and to say simply, "I love you and I'm proud you are my son or daughter."

It felt good to say it. And it still does.

51. Randy

Once we had living in our house a big red and white collie named Randy. During his later years he grew lethargic and spent most of the day lying on the kitchen floor directly in front of the refrigerator. We never discovered just why he chose that place unless he wanted to be there in case something dropped out. After all, when you reach the human equivalent of ninety-eight years old, you prefer to have your food drop on you instead of having to go after it.

Everything in our house seemed to revolve around Randy. We couldn't take a vacation until we lined up a dog-sitter—because Randy refused to get in the car to go anyplace. Visitors were obliged to step over him when they entered the kitchen, for no amount of coaxing could persuade him to move from his spot in front of the refrigerator. Even our cat, Mrs. Robinson, could not budge him. One day she stalked through the kitchen and finding him blocking the way, proceeded to walk right over him, deliberately stepping on his face as she crossed his bulky form. He never budged.

When Randy wanted out he would slowly stagger to his feet and walk to the front door. (He never used the back door. That was for children and cats.) He would scratch on the door to draw our attention. If someone did not immediately open the door, he would, in a very dignified way, lift his back leg and wet on the floor. He would then return to his place in front of the refrigerator. We soon learned that whenever Randy got to his feet he meant business. He was king of the household.

He was also king of the neighborhood. When we let Randy out the front door he would walk slowly down the driveway to the middle of the street, turn right, and head for the fireplug on the corner. Head up. Feet padding regally on the asphalt. Big tail waving majestically behind him. He had the unmistakable air of royalty.

His presence in the street was the signal for every little dog in the neighborhood to come dashing out to bark at him. They would stand on the sidewalk, the hair on their backs raised like bristles, yapping in animosity and envy. They all knew Randy was king.

It never fazed him. After visiting the fireplug he would retrace his steps. The little dogs would increase their yapping, but he never even granted them the satisfaction of a sneer. He would walk slowly to the front door, scratch once, enter, and return to his place in front of the refrigerator.

Randy had learned the spiritual principle of dominion—a principle very few Christians have mastered. He knew who he was and refused to settle for anything less. In a world full of yappers, he set his eyes on his purpose and never, until the day he died, allowed himself to be distracted.

Today's saints need to learn from Randy and recognize they are royalty—heirs of God and joint heirs with Christ. The dominion God gave Adam in the garden of Eden has been literally restored to His saints through Jesus Christ.

For most of us, though, that's a theory which works only until someone—or something—barks from the sidelines. As a result we can't even reach the fireplug, much less go beyond to the place of peace and provision.

There is no need to be distracted by the yappers of depression, demons, and disease. Instead, we should do as Kenneth Copeland, who, when distracted by a sneeze, once threw up his hands and said, "Praise God, I'm catching a healing."

The victory is ours. All we need to do is walk in it.

52. Just Don't Say It Very Loud

The highlight of Handel's *Messiah* is "The Hallelujah Chorus." Here the entire orchestra, chorus, and soloists join in a rousing tribute of praise unexcelled in western music. Although he used some of his previously composed music, Georg Friedrich Handel sketched and scored the entire composition in an incredible twenty-one days.

An old story states that when the oratorio was performed before the king, and he heard the choir and orchestra join in those mighty "hallelujahs," he was so moved he stood to his feet—meaning the entire congregation had to follow suit. Lately it has been suggested (with what truth I do not know) that the king was on his way to relieve the royal kidney. If so, what surprise he must have experienced when he realized the rest of the audience loyally rose as well. Whatever the reason, contemporary audiences still rise when the magnificent chorus is reached in the rendition. Although I fear some feel the rising is a terrible inconvenience, I find it impossible to remain seated—and only with restrained deference to those around, do I keep myself from raising my arms and joining in singing those mighty notes of praise.

The word "hallelujah" comes from the Hebrew language. Depending on its spelling it means "Praise ye Jehovah" or "Praise ye Elohim" (the two Hebrew words for God). Translated into English it means "Praise the Lord."

The only truly international word among Christians is the word "hallelujah." It is just as understandable behind the Iron Curtain, in the Orient, or in South America as it is in America or Israel. To all it means, "Praise the Lord."

Ironically, the Christian church seldom uses phrases like "hallelujah" or "praise the Lord" any more. Ministers tell me the terms have been "vulgarized" by their common usage in less sophisticated Christian circles. Most churches still approve of their use in music, but would be horrified if some exhilarated worshiper were to suddenly leap to his feet in the back of the sanctuary and shout, "Hallelujah!"

The only acceptable term in most churches is the term "amen"—and it is acceptable only at the close of a long prayer.

I remember a particular man in one of the churches I used to attend who would sometimes say "amen" in the middle of the sermon. It flustered the preacher who thought the man was trying to signal it was time to close the sermon. Besides, even the preacher didn't think he was saying anything worthy of an "amen." We later discovered the man hadn't been listening to the sermon at all. He was sitting in the back reading his Bible and got so excited he would occasionally break out into a spontaneous "amen!" After a few Sundays of this the other worshipers began avoiding him like he had bad breath and he soon moved on. Just where nobody seemed to care.

Recently I've been campaigning for a return, in our staid and sophisticated services, of the terms "Praise the Lord" and

Just Don't Say It Very Loud

"Hallelujah." Most worshipers leave such mutterings up to the priest or preacher, but true worship consists of everyone joining in—not just under their breath or "to themselves."

Jackie gave me a tambourine for Christmas one year. She said if I was going to enter fully into worship I should do it in a biblical manner. Since I don't do very well on the loud cymbals or high sounding cymbals, she thought I could at least handle the timbrel, or tambourine. Sadly, there are very few places who will accept me when they see (or rather, hear) me coming. It seems that tambourines just aren't "in" these days.

I remember hearing about a girl who brought a small harp to church and wanted to play it during the hymns. The usher told her their church didn't allow harps. "Oh, oh," she said, backing out in a hurry, "you folks are really going to have trouble one of these days."

Maybe the reason G.F. Handel was able to shout "Hallelujah" was he knew "the Lord God omnipotent reigneth." I have a feeling when others discover that, they, too, will shout: "Praise the Lord!"

53. *Ready for the Old Volks Home*

Recently I've been studying about my "place" in the Body of Christ. Some, the Bible teacher said knowingly, are arms, others are legs, some are ears, and others noses. One friend says he's the fat—useless except when burned up. All of us should seek our place, however, and cheerfully abide there.

I'm not quite sure how to find my place, though, except through the process of elimination. One thing I know I am not—and that's a mechanic. Some people are born mechanics. Me? Every time I take something apart, someone else has to put it back together again.

For almost a year the ignition on my old Volkswagen had been out of whack. Even though I had the spare part in the glove compartment, it was easier to take the back off the ignition switch and start the car by crossing the wires with a penny. This caused a lot of sparks, and sometimes smoke, but it worked. The penny found a permanent resting place on the dashboard.

Then, after a year of this method, I began to notice an unusual amount of sparking and smoking. Suddenly, it failed to work any more. Naturally I didn't know why. But it did seem time to replace the broken ignition. That's where all the trouble began.

The inside of the steering column of a VW is composed of hundreds of tiny screws, washers, and other things which fall out the minute you take the steering wheel off. After three hours of trying to get it back together (I had, in the process, discovered it was not necessary to take the steering wheel off to replace the ignition part), I gave up and pushed it three blocks to Honest Fred, the foreign car expert. Fred took one look at the bag of springs and washers, looked at me sadly, and shook his head. I knew, all the time he was talking, that he was itemizing the bill in his head.

I returned home and decided since I had my hands already covered with grease, this was a good time to drain the radiator in our Chevrolet station wagon. We were planning a vacation trip north and I wanted to add antifreeze.

Any fool can drain a radiator. All you have to do is twist the drain cock and out comes the water. But when I twisted the drain cock on our six-year-old car, out came the drain cock—leaving a gaping hole in the bottom of the radiator. Fortunately, Fred also works on domestic cars, so I stuck bubblegum over the hole, filled the radiator, and made haste to the garage.

Fred took the radiator off and brazed the hole shut—forever. Now all I have to do to drain the radiator is turn the car upside down. Fred also agreed, with something akin to a wicked grin, to add this additional charge to my bill.

Even when things are accompanied by directions, I can't seem to get them together. The kids still rib me about last Christmas, when I spent all afternoon trying to assemble a Sears Roebuck bicycle which had come with each part individually wrapped. After tearing all the meat off my knuckles and thinking some very un-Christmas thoughts, I asked my neighbor to help me. (At that time I didn't think Jackie's suggestion that I call Honest Fred was very funny.) The front wheel never did turn correctly when you turned the handlebars, but the bike looked great when it was propped up against the side of the house.

Then, two days after the Super Bowl game, I finally got around to putting Jackie's shelves in her pantry. She wanted fourteen narrow shelves thirty-two inches long. It wasn't until I sawed all fourteen of them with a hand saw which the kids had left out in the rain, that I discovered I had been reading my yardstick upside down. The shelves were all twenty-three inches long rather than thirty-two.

That evening I walked into my son's bedroom where he was putting his electric rocket launcher together.

"Need some help, son?" I smiled.

I should have expected his answer when he looked up with a half-frightened stare and said, "Uh, no thanks, dad. I guess I can tear it up by myself."

Maybe I'm supposed to be a rib or a thigh bone. Fingers I am not.

54. A World Full of Runners

He was watery-eyed, fiftyish, and had tiny red veins which showed through the skin on his nose. I was engrossed in a magazine article as he settled wearily in the seat beside me on the plane.

After fumbling with his seat belt he sighed, reached in his coat, and withdrew a pocket calendar. I glanced at it and then turned back and stared. I thought my travel schedule was full, but I could see nearly every day of the month on his calendar marked with names like: Dallas, Richmond, St. Louis, Minneapolis, Fresno, Omaha. . . .

He glanced up and caught me looking. Smiling weakly as he closed the calendar and put it in his coat pocket, he commented, "I wonder what the weather is in Chicago this morning."

We chatted a few minutes as the plane slipped into the early morning sky. I asked him what he did for a living that kept him on the move all the time.

"I sell pharmaceuticals," he said. "But if you really want to know the truth, I'm a runner."

In the jargon of the street, "runner" has a particular meaning. But this man looked like anything but a dope pusher. "Runner?" I asked.

"That's right," he said, settling back in his seat with a slump of resignation. "I'm running away from my family, myself, and any other form of reality. Stay with me three hours and I'll be drunk, too."

I closed the magazine. Anyone that honest was ready to talk.

"Most guys like me are running," he said, speaking so softly I could barely hear him over the roar of the big jet engines. "On the surface I'm successful. Last year I cleared eighty grand. I've got a big estate in the country and a 'man' who drives me to the airport. But my family don't respect me. And why should they? I don't respect myself."

"What about your friends?"

He tilted his head and looked at me through squinted eyes, half smiling. "You've gotta be kidding. All I have are a bunch of salesmen, every one of them an SOB who would do anything to get my job. I've gotta keep running. If I don't, one of them will catch up with me and cut my throat."

He gulped the cocktail the stewardess had put before him and motioned for another. "Can you imagine what it's like to spend the night in two hundred different motel rooms each year? Alone, or with a bottle?"

He turned and looked at me. "You're not a runner, are you?"

"I used to be," I said. "But I've been caught from behind and discovered a satisfaction and security I never dreamed existed."

"Oh yeah? Who were you running from? Some dame?"

"No, I was running from God," I said softly.

"You must be some kind of a nut," he said harshly, gulping his second cocktail.

"Not a nut," I said. "I used to be a fool. But all that's changed now. Now I'm happy. And free."

"You're serious, aren't you?" he said, turning toward me as far as his seat belt would allow.

"Dead serious," I said. "Do you want to know the key to all this?"

"Do you think God made me sit down beside you?" he asked, his eyes filling with moisture. "No one else knows how much I dreaded starting another week."

We talked for an hour. When the stewardess came back to ask if he wanted more to drink he waved her away. Turning to me, he said, "I don't think I'll need any more of that, do you?"

"Not if you stay as serious as you are now," I said.

The plane rolled to a stop at the terminal and we both ran to meet connections. He to Chicago, me back home. I'll never see him again. Not on earth, anyway. But I'll see others, thousands of them. They are the successful failures. But only a few are honest enough—or desperate enough—to reach out in truth and grasp help when it sits down beside them. The rest will keep running.

55. I'm More Than a Man With a Droopy Eyelid

It's odd, you know, how we usually describe other people by their defects. A friend of mine asked if I had seen Mr. Williams. I know several men by that name and asked, "Which Mr. Williams?"

"Oh," he replied quickly, "the man with one arm."

Surely there must be a better way to remember people than by their imperfections.

"The man with the wart on his nose."

"The guy who drinks too much."

"The old lady who limps."

"The kid who stutters."

We are constantly picking out flaws—and missing the beauty around us.

I learned my lesson about describing people by their imperfections when I met Eunice Wood. Eunice is a tall, middle-aged woman with very irregular teeth. They tend to protrude even when she closes her mouth. Every time someone mentioned Eunice, the image of buck teeth flashed on my mind.

Then last month Eunice's husband, Ira, had a heart attack. Ira was a big, strong truck driver, but for a few days even the doctors feared he might die. I went to the hospital to visit him. Eunice was standing beside his bed, her tender hands caressing his sick body, her face bathed in love as she whispered faith and encouragement in his ear. As I looked, I saw on her face the countenance of an angel.

The next day I was telling someone about Eunice's husband. "Who's Eunice?" he asked. Before I could think, I heard myself describing her as the woman with the angelic face.

We are all creations of His likeness. I have since determined to make a list of every person I encounter, either on paper or in my mind, and describe the one quality in him or her which is not only the most God-like, but which can also serve as a description. Warts. Stutters. Twisted hands. Bald heads. Crooked or missing limbs. Accents. We all have defects. But when we look beyond them, as God does, we can see His image in us all.

56. You've Sure Got a Bunch of Sick Folks in Your Church

What Spirit-filled believer, freshly catapulted into a new dimension of personal honesty—only to be badly stung by the sharp reactions of those still bound in tradition—has not wanted to cry out with Iago in Shakespeare's *Othello:* "Take note, take note, O World, to be direct and honest is not safe"?

Iago was right. Honesty can get you killed—or kicked out of office. The honest man is a threat to all those around him who are not honest, be it politics, business, or the church. It's one thing to tell the truth; but to "let it all hang out" is more than most folks can stand.

Last year some old friends arrived at our house on a Sunday afternoon. Traveling with them was the man's mother who, although a staunch church member, was totally uninitiated when it came to attending our free-wheeling Sunday night service. In fact, it was almost too much for her.

Our friends reacted well. They had been in "body life"

meetings before. The hugging, happiness, and hand-clapping didn't seem to bother them. But the mother, an older woman who was a member of a very sophisticated church in Richmond, Virginia, sat through the two-hour service with a look of stark dismay on her face.

The initial shock came when she entered the building and found people—instead of sitting coldly in pews staring forward and listening to solemn music—milling about, laughing, talking, and hugging one another. I couldn't help but sympathize with her, for many times in my days of formalism I had wanted to mount the pulpit before the service and shout, "Stop all that loving, you magpies, it's time to be religious."

There were other problems. Besides being the only woman in the building wearing hat and gloves, she had to sit beside a burly young man with a huge red beard who was dressed in overalls and shaking a tambourine.

This was church?

But it wasn't the clapping, prophecy, or spontaneous testimonies that bothered her most. It was the honesty.

About halfway through the service there was a call for ministry. "If there are any here with great burdens, we want to pray for you," the presiding elder said. "Perhaps you're not able to get along with your husband or wife. Maybe you're out of work and filled with fear for the future. Perhaps you're depressed, sick, or unable to cope with life. Are you bothered by evil spirits? Are you being tempted sexually? Have you been considering suicide? If so, stand up and let the Body of Christ gather around you, lay hands on you, and pray."

More than half the congregation stood. The rest reached out to touch, and entered into a time of free, vocal prayer. Some of those standing responded with tears, others with laughter. One or two even shouted as they received deliverance. Others just stood silently, accepting by faith what God had promised.

After the service, as we sat around our dining room table

munching crackers and cheese, the mother finally spoke up.

"Ah . . . that was an unusual service tonight."

"Not really," I said casually. "Although I guess it was different from the type of service you have in Richmond."

She searched for the proper words. "Was that usual—all those people standing up for prayer like that?"

"What do you mean?"

"I mean," she said, a bit bolder now, "I can't imagine my pastor ever asking people to admit they couldn't get along with their husbands, had sexual temptations, or were considering suicide. We just don't do things like that in our church."

"What if he did give that kind of invitation?" I probed.

"Oh, no one would dare stand up," she said quickly.

Then she delivered the *coup de grace*. "You must have an awful lot of sick people in your church."

I could feel my face growing hot. But I choked down the cutting retorts and sat thinking. Silently. She was right. We do have an awful lot of sick people in our church.

But so does every church. The difference is honesty—and people who run the risk of condemnation by admitting their need, and asking for help. But after all, are churches to be resorts for saints—or hospitals for sinners?

The villain Iago concluded, under Othello's prodding, that honesty must be steeped in wisdom "for honesty's a fool and loses that it works for."

Granted, there are some things better left unsaid. That's the wise part of honesty. But true healing comes only when we become transparent—even if we have to die in the process.

57. Here, Let Me Show You How

Someone once said he'd never seen a self-made man who didn't show evidence of unskilled labor.

I don't know about self-made men, but I am learning a lot about unskilled labor. In fact, I are one.

Back in college I had a summer construction job, working as an assistant to a notorious carpenter called Lying John Williams. Lying John didn't take much to college kids. I remember one time he told me that although I might be able to quote Shakespeare and spell Charlemagne, I would never make a good carpenter. Part of his evaluation was based on the fact I didn't chew tobacco. The rest seemed to come from the way I held my hammer, which was up close to the head rather than out on the end where I could hit a nail with authority.

It was Lying John who taught me about true measurements, however. The second day on the job he handed me a stack of lumber and said, "Saw me ten boards exactly seventy-two inches long."

I pulled out my measuring tape and measured the first board, marking it with the square. I sawed it right on the line. Then I took the second board, laid it across the saw horses, put the first board on top, and marked it off. When I finished sawing I laid the third board on the sawhorses, measured with the second board, and so on until I finished all ten boards.

When Lying John reappeared he took all ten boards and stood them up on end. I couldn't believe my eyes. Every board was a quarter-inch longer than the next board—and the tenth board was two and a half inches longer than the original board.

Lying John let them fall to the ground, picked up the saw and handed it back. "Get to work, College Kid," he said, "and remember, to get a true measure, always use the same stick."

All this came to mind a while ago when a crew of carpenters moved in to tear the roof off the back part of our old house and begin a second-floor addition. Knowing these men were paid by the hour, I determined to speed things up by getting topside to help. That's where the unskilled part all came to the surface again.

Even though it was my roof we were working on, I was assigned my old role as a carpenter's helper. The tobacco-chewing foreman, who looked and acted strangely like Lying John, called me "Bub" and never even gave me a chance to hold the hammer. The only tool he let me use was a broom—used for sweeping up the gravel from the topside of the exposed ceiling.

Feeling the need to boss someone around, I asked my sixteen-year-old son to assist me. The first thing I did, after he joined me on the roof, was to warn him what I would do if he clumsily missed his step and busted a hole in the ceiling. The second thing I did was turn around, miss the 2 x 8 with my foot, and stick it through the exposed ceiling board—directly over his bedroom.

I figured I had saved enough money for the day and spent the rest of the afternoon doing my specialty, picking up bent nails from the patio.

Later that afternoon, without the carpenters around to make me feel inferior, I took my son back out to show him how to saw up the discarded roof trusses. In quick order I (1) stepped on a nail, (2) dropped a huge plank on my foot, and (3) sawed through the cord on the electric saw.

I decided it was time to go inside and write something. I left my son on the patio. When I peeked through the curtains I saw him skillfully driving nails into a 2 x 8—holding the hammer all the way down at the end of the handle and hitting the nails with authority.

Unlike his unskilled dad, he just might make a good carpenter. Even if he doesn't chew tobacco.

58. Don't Just Do Something

As long as I can remember, I have been around people who told me to hurry up. As a child it was my parents and older brothers who called me a "slowpoke." Then it was a series of coaches who told me to "hustle." Drill sergeants told me "Get the lead out!" and college professors demanded I have my papers in on time or suffer from bad grades. Now I am constantly fighting the battle of deadlines with publishers and editors who scream for copy. Everybody, it seems, is in a hurry.

Even those in my circle of Christian friends seem to be afflicted with this sense of haste. Since my clock has already been wound to the breaking point, I sometimes wonder if that first definition of a fanatic might not be correct: A fanatic is one who has lost his way and redoubled his efforts.

I recall one of my fellow seminary students asking one of the wiser professors if he thought pentecostals would get to heaven. He chuckled and said, "Yes, if they don't run by it."

THE LAST WORD

Satan thrives on haste, while the Holy Spirit delights in patience. The only time Jesus pictures God in a hurry is when He is running to meet a lost son returning from a far country. Even in raising dead Lazarus, Jesus seemed to be in no hurry.

Perhaps Pascal had something when he said, several hundred years ago, "All troubles of man come from his not knowing how to sit still." It was this same concept that caused Will Rogers to say that one of his ambitions was to step out into the middle of a busy street, hold up his hands, stop all traffic, and tell everyone who wasn't going anyplace to go home.

It's easy for the hurry-up person to get out of the will of God. Prophecies that say, "Do it now or it will be too late," are invariably false prophecies. And people who impatiently insist that certain manifestations accompany certain spiritual experiences—or the experience isn't real—are never on target with God's purpose. When the Holy Spirit does the ministering, there is no need to manipulate a person to respond—either by speaking in tongues individually, or by shouting "amen" as a crowd.

The gifts of the Spirit, which are things we *do*, are effective only when the fruit of the Spirit, which are things we *are*, are present. Therefore Paul says that even if you speak in tongues, prophesy, or give accurate words of knowledge, all is useless unless you love.

James Garfield, who was later president of the United States, was principal at Hiram College in Ohio when a hurry-up father enrolled his son. The father came to Fairfield asking if there was some kind of shortcut that would get his son through college more quickly and out into the world of moneymaking. Garfield's answer remains a classic.

"Certainly, but it all depends on what you want to make of your boy. When God wants to make an oak tree, He takes one hundred years. When He wants to make a squash, He requires only two months."

Don't Just Do Something

Patience, I am learning, is a matter of relativity. No matter how fast I go, there is always someone around who thinks I should go faster. Like the red-faced guy with white knuckles who seems to always be behind me when the traffic light turns from red to green. The blast from his horn tells me far more about him than about me.

Yet few people seem to have time to stop and listen when I tell them speed is not the answer to all our problems. In fact, some of my friends insist we need to hurry up with things like building church buildings and other grand programs. Wouldn't it be awful if Jesus were to come tomorrow and we hadn't completed the task?

I was one of the few people in the nation who cheered when the speed limits were lowered to 55 mph. I enjoy looking out the windows and stopping to smell the flowers. Of course, it's hard to do that when everyone behind you is blowing his horn, shaking his fist, and growling into his CB microphone about a "turtle in the road."

When the Hebrews came to the edge of the Red Sea after leaving Egypt, they began to act like cattle who, walking head down before a winter wind, come to a strand of barbed wire. There, on the banks of the sea, they murmured against Moses who had led them—so they said—out in the desert to die.

"Don't just stand there," I can hear one young Israelite shout at Moses, "do something."

But Moses had heard God speak from the burning bush. He knew the very essence of God was caught up in His name: not "I do" but "I Am."

"You've got it backward," Moses told the muttering crowd. "What you should have said is, 'Don't just do something, stand there.'"

Recently I spent a week with my father who was in his eighty-sixth year. His leg muscles don't function very well any more, leaving him dependent on his wheelchair and walker to get him where he wants to go.

"All I need is folks around me who are willing to be patient," he said one morning, shuffling from the bedroom to the kitchen. "I know where I'm going and how to get there. It just takes me a little longer than before."

Well, I know a lot of folks moving ten times faster who have no idea where they are going.

Jesus never seemed to be in a hurry, yet He accomplished everything He set out to do in three years. Of course He didn't let a lot of foolish things consume His time either. That means while I am being deliberate, I must be diligent also.

My father has taught me the lesson. "The secret to enjoying going slower, is to start sooner."

59. *I Found It*

As far back as I can recall, I have been afraid of the unknown.
When I was a boy we used to take long trips from Florida to visit
aunts and uncles in Kentucky and Indiana. Motels were
nonexistent in those days, so we spent our nights on the road in
tourist homes—big houses in small Southern towns where a
widow or a retired couple would rent out rooms for the night.

It was always a terrifying experience, carrying the suitcases up
the front steps, peering into the strange bathrooms at the end of
the dark hall, and lying in bed at night listening for the footsteps
of whatever was destined to "get me" in the darkness.

Equally frightening was the experience of driving into a
strange city, especially if we arrived at night with the rain
peppering the windshield. I was always glad if I could ride in the
front seat so I could huddle close to my dad, who was the one
connecting link with the only place in the world where I was not
afraid—the big house back in the orange grove in Vero Beach.

THE LAST WORD

The fears stayed with me as I grew older. When Jackie and I married and drove from Florida to Texas, it was the first time either of us had been away from home on our own. The first night our car broke down in Pensacola. It was dark and raining. I forced myself to do what was necessary—but what I really wanted to do was run all the way home.

In Fort Worth I found a job driving a city bus. I would get up before dawn and drive into the city to work—scared to death. Except for working for my dad in the groves, a summer job with the county construction crew, and washing dishes in the college dining hall, it was my first job. I stayed scared all the time.

All the other people in the city seemed busy and secure. What I didn't know was they were mostly like me—afraid, insecure, and always on the verge of panic.

The only place I knew where I felt secure, even though I was married and working and attending graduate school, was back home with my parents, my brothers and sister, my dog, and my bed.

Then the old home place changed hands—and part of me died. The old pastor at the church moved away and a new man came on the scene who was more of a go-getter than a friend. Friends and loved ones died. Gradually I began to realize that if I was to find security I would have to look in another dimension—the dimension of the eternal.

In the kingdom of God I have found all I was looking for in the dimension of the world—plus more. It started with a relationship with the Heavenly Father which is more real than I had with my own daddy. It continued with the joy of knowing Christ as my friend and older brother. It climaxed with the joy of being filled with the Holy Spirit. It is being completed as the church, the visible expression ot the Body of Christ on earth, gathers around me in a community of loving, caring brothers and sisters.

It is this kind of perfect love which has, at last, cast out my fear.

Excuse me
and
God bless
you!

60. One Life to Share

I often wonder whatever happened to Kenneth Bookout and Joe Springer. Kenneth and Joe were fellow freshmen with me at Mercer University twenty-six years ago.

It's strange that I should think of them now, since I knew them so slightly during that year at college. Kenneth transferred to another school at the end of his freshman year, and Joe disappeared a year later. I've never heard of either of them since; yet, just this morning as I was taking a shower, they popped into my mind. Strange, but they both had a powerful influence on my life.

Kenneth lived on the other end of old Sherwood Hall, the freshman dormitory located on the beautiful campus operated by the Georgia Baptist Convention in Macon. He was the only freshman—for that matter, the only guy on campus—who wore a pin stripe suit. Extremely studious, quiet, and deeply spiritual, the credits under his annual picture listed: Life Service Band,

213

Choir, and Religious Education Association. That was a far cry from my list of important activities: R.O.T.C., ATO Greek letter social fraternity, varsity basketball and track, and Student Government Association. These marked me as a BMOC—Big Man On Campus—while Kenneth and Joe were like the faded flowers on the wallpaper in the dean's office.

I never talked to Kenneth—not a single time. He would remember me only as the loudmouth from the other wing who was always leading the hallrunners in practical jokes. A favorite was to stick a firecracker in the keyhole of his door. Another was to set fire to a piece of paper, stick it under his door and shout, "Fire! Fire!" When he opened the door, book in hand and peering over his glasses, we'd douse him with a bucket of water before running.

Shy and preoccupied, he preferred staying in his room at night, reading his Bible, rather than joining us in a panty raid on the girls' dorm.

Rumor said he once walked head-on into a huge pecan tree in front of the library because he had his head down in a book. Picking himself up from the ground, he supposedly smiled, and said, "Excuse me and God bless you," and continued on to class.

Joe Springer lived two doors down the hall from me. Like Kenneth, he was a Baptist ministerial student. One arm was slightly deformed and he always looked like he had put his coat on without taking out the coat hanger. While my weekends were spent on fraternity parties, Joe spent his weekends preaching at a small country church.

Unless I was involved in a short-sheet escapade, or was smearing vaseline on their doorknobs, I stayed as far away from both boys as I could. They disturbed me. Yet, even though I have not seen or heard of either in more than two and a half decades, I am still affected by their influence.

I must have had thousands of conversations my freshman

year, but I remember only one. It was a short conversation with Joe Springer one winter afternoon. I had come in from basketball practice and spotted him through the open door of his room as I walked down the hall of the dorm. He was propped up in bed reading his Bible. For some reason I stopped and talked, for deep inside I respected him.

"Jamie," he said seriously, "God needs some real men in the ministry. Why don't you give him your life?"

I don't remember my answer. I imagine I laughed it off. But I never could shake the question. It burned deep in my heart. It was like the time we tied Kenneth's shoelaces together while he was reading a book in the dining hall. When he stood up he lost his balance and crashed to the floor. His only reply, given with a shy smile, was, "Hey, that's a great trick, fellows."

God, how that seared my heart!

Like I said, I often wonder whatever became of them. This is certain, however: they were walking to the beat of a different drummer. They must be far, far down the road by now. I hope so, for their small witness went a long way in pointing me toward Christ.

The romance of the military ball has faded. Newsclippings of my campus activities are yellowed. Even my fraternity pin, that treasured Maltese cross with the diamond in the middle, is lost. Yet, haunting me today, even as I take a shower, are the faces of the two boys who dared to be different. Although they never knew it, they helped change my life.

I am grateful.

61. *The Love Bug*

According to my friend, Costa Deir, there is a vast difference between love and infatuation. Infatuation is an emotion which controls us. Love is an act of the will—which we control.

Costa, who was born in Ramla when Israel was then Palestine, often talks of the old customs of the Mideast. There young men and women did not date. That kind of contact only stirred the emotions. Instead, they waited until they were ready to marry and by an act of their will, loved the one chosen by their parents.

In *Fiddler on the Roof*, after twenty-five years of marriage, Tevye finally asks Golde, "Do you love me?"

"The first time I met you was on our wedding day. . . . But my father and my mother said we'd learn to love each other."

"Do you love me?"

Golde answers:

"For twenty-five years I've lived with him, fought with him, starved with him.

Twenty-five years my bed is his;

If that's not love, what is?"

We westerners know very little of that depth of love. We speak glibly of falling in and out of love. But according to the Bible, love is something you do, not something you cannot help—like catching the flu.

I "fell in love" as a teenager in high school. I later married that same girl. Now I realize I didn't love her. I was only infatuated by her. It has taken me years to learn to love her—an act of my will.

I was explaining this to our fourteen-year-old daughter and she asked, "You mean you could love any girl as much as you love me?"

I answered, "When your older sisters and brothers were born I loved them. But I did not love you because I did not know you. When you arrived, several years later, I willed myself to love you as much as I loved them. I did not love you simply because I had to. The nurse could have handed me any baby in the nursery and I could have willed myself to love that baby. Fortunately she handed me the one your mother had given birth to—and I chose to love you, because I wanted to."

I went ahead to explain how my parents, after having had four sons, adopted a tiny baby girl. They willed themselves to love her just as much as they loved their own children. In turn, I willed myself to love her as much as I love my brothers.

The question continually comes up: can a man love two women with equal love? Of course he can, if he wills himself to it. He can love a dozen women as much as he loves his wife. But in the Christian context of monogamy, we, by an act of our will, determine to love only one person supremely. We are not forced to, nor is it a capricious thing that says a married man cannot help it if he falls in love with a woman other than his wife. He can help it. It is his decision.

I can love whomever I please, and to what depth I please Love is not conditioned by how much I am loved back in return, or even whether I am loved in return. It is something I do of my own free will. It is not a whim or fancy which "comes on me" as the song writers suggest. That is infatuation. An emotion. Love is something I alone control.

Love is a deliberate act. In fact, I am commanded by the Bible to love. And if I cannot, if the task is too hard, then there is an escape. "The love of God is shed abroad in our hearts by the Holy Ghost which is given unto us" (Romans 5:5).

Therefore I can love my wife even if she does not love me back in return—and love her supremely. I can love my parents, my enemies, even my neighbor. I do it as an act of my will. And that makes it much more meaningful.

62. Grow Old Along With Me

It started about three years ago. In order to read fine print, I had to hold it at arm's length. My ophthalmologist insisted it was not a lack of faith. "After you reach forty, the muscles in your eyes begin to lose their elasticity," he said. To help me along, he put me in reading glasses.

My eye muscles aren't the only ones which don't stretch very well any more. I have a similar problem with my memory muscle—especially when it comes to remembering names of people. At such times my brain resembles an ancient rubber band, hardened and corroded, ready to snap at the slightest exertion.

My big problem comes with people who grab my hand in some public place and say, "I'll bet you don't remember me, do you?"

I squint at them through my unstretchable eyes and usually say something stupid like, "I may forget your name, but I'd never forget a face like that."

THE LAST WORD

I used to lie and say, "Sure, I remember you." But there are just enough brazen people who answer, "Then who am I?" I've been cured of that approach.

I keep hearing about folks who can memorize phone books. But I can't even look up a number and remember it long enough to dial the phone. I have to keep glancing back and forth from the dial to the phone—and that's quite a feat when you've forgotten where you placed your glasses and have to hold the phone book at arm's length and dial at the same time.

My wife is my best defense. When we are together and I see someone approaching whose name I have forgotten, I quickly introduce them first. "Well, well, look who's here. Have you met my wife, Jackie?"

She is much more adept at pulling out names, at which time I can step back into the conversation with, "Dan's an old friend, honey. We met in the Hong Kong airport six years ago."

Recently I've found myself responding to the "betcha-don't-remember-me" people by saying, "I guess you don't know, but I suffered brain damage when I was forty. . . ." Which is about as close to the truth as I can come without saying, "Not only have I forgotten your name, but I have forgotten where I am. What city is this, anyway?"

Then one Tuesday morning the very worst thing which could happen—happened. I was having breakfast with Bruce Morgan in a back booth at Sambo's. We were just finishing our conversation when I looked up and saw a short, sixtyish man approaching, holding his coffee cup.

I instantly recognized him as my Scottish friend who attends the church, Andy Allison.

"Andy," I beamed, pumping his hand. "It's good to see you. Meet Bruce Morgan."

"Delighted to meet a Scotchman," Bruce said.

Andy sat down and we chatted for a few moments, then Bruce said to me, "By the way, who was that other Scotchman who testified at the church last Sunday? I thought his name was Andy Allison."

I suddenly felt sick. Very sick. The man next to me was not Andy at all. He was Wayne Roberts, a quiet humble fellow who brings his wife to the church services every week in a wheelchair—and far more Irish than Scotch. He was so pleased that I had let him sit next to me that he was willing to put up with my calling him by someone else's name. Oh, Lord, what now?

In good military fashion, I created a diversion. First a coughing spell, then I turned over my water. We were all on our feet and it was time to go.

I grabbed Bruce's arm and tried to pull him away, but not until he got in a cheery, "Good to see you, Andy. Nice to talk to a Scotchman."

Outside in the car, fighting back waves of nausea, I looked up and saw Mr. Roberts sitting at the counter with his coffee, waving at me.

The next morning at the elders' meeting I confessed to my peers. They encouraged me. I was just growing old and my brain muscle had lost its elasticity. Besides, one of the elders said, he had talked to Mr. Roberts yesterday afternoon, and this explained why he was now speaking with a Scotch brogue.

The other guys thought that was hilarious. I wanted to cry.

So, here we are at the end of another year. My teeth are breaking off. My eyes are going bad. And my memory muscle isn't stretching as well as it used to. But I want you to know the real me is still very much alive in Jesus.

Cosmetics may hide the wrinkles, a toupee can cover a bald spot, and contact lenses can fool the public. But the only defense against a poor memory is the truth. I won't be offended by your brass, if you won't be offended by my brain.

"Now, what was your name again?"

63. But We've Always Done It This Way

Like 200 million other lazy Americans, I am a creature of routine.

Most of these are good routines. I like to brush my teeth as soon as I crawl out of bed in the morning. I simply cannot tolerate "tooth film" and "tongue fuzz."

A Sunday afternoon nap is so much of a "must" that I invariably get sleepy as soon as we finish the Sunday noon meal—even if I am at someone else's house.

There are hundreds of other routines. I take my shoes off when I sit down at the typewriter. I resist Saturday night invitations, preferring to spend a quiet evening at home with the family—or by myself. I answer the telephone only if there is no one else in the house—and sometimes not then. Our listed number rings at my secretary's home. When the phone does ring at my home, even if I am standing beside it in the kitchen, I step aside to let Jackie answer. It's just one of my routines.

But there is a problem. Routines become habits. Habits are but one step removed from ruts. And everyone knows a rut is nothing but a grave with both ends knocked out.

Lately I've been looking at these routines in my life. I always lather from my left arm first when I step in the shower. When I raise my arms in worship, I always turn my palms in. Never out. I always sit in the same chair at church on Sunday morning. In fact, when I came in several Sundays ago and someone had taken "my chair," I lost my joy and had a hard time worshiping—even with my palms turned in.

There's something wrong with all this. Slowly, yet certainly, I am hardening into an old wineskin—unable to contain the new wine of change which is the freshness and spontaneity of the Holy Spirit.

So, I have made one of my infamous lists. Some of my routines do not need changing—like praying with my kids every night before they go to bed. But the vast majority are simply ruts into which I've fallen. In an effort to put new elasticity into my aging wineskin, I've determined to change. But it doesn't come easy.

Recently we had Sunday afternoon visitors. They came for lunch and stayed until time for the evening service. In the car on the way to church that night, Jackie chided me.

"Why didn't you just excuse yourself and go on to bed?"

"But I was breaking the routine of having to take a nap."

"Well, you took one anyway. Right in your chair. I was so embarrassed—all that snoring. . . ."

I cannot understand it. I never get sleepy on Tuesday afternoon.

Last Saturday night Jackie insisted I take her out for Chinese food. "You've been out of town all week and all I've done is cook for these children. I've been dreaming of Chinese food for two days."

I agreed, but I wasn't happy about it. Saturday nights are my nights to stay home.

On the way to the Dragon Lady Restaurant our fourteen-year-old Sandy was sitting between her mother and me in the front seat. She was caught in the crossfire of silent tension and finally said, "Daddy, you sure are grumpy. You're going to spoil our whole evening. I need to pray for you."

She put her hand on my leg and prayed out loud as I mumbled about the traffic and expense of eating out. But the prayer helped. And so did her painful expose that I was more like a rock than clay in the Potter's hands.

Psychologists talk about "adjusting" to unpleasant situations—like having to sit in the smoking section when it burns your eyes and stinks up your clothes, not getting your morning cup of coffee, or having to sleep on a lumpy mattress at the motel—without screaming about your rights being violated.

"Adjust" is a good word, but I prefer the biblical concept of being "transformed."

There is a problem with transformation, however. It means I can't complain any more if my routine is broken. It means I've been bought with a price and don't belong to myself. It means I can't gripe if things don't go my way.

Christians may get old—but that's no reason we have to get stiff. So I've grown a mustache—just for the change. And will probably shave it off when I (and others) get used to it. And I'm waiting until after I shave to brush my teeth in the morning. I've even started sitting in a new place in church.

A young man wrote me recently saying, "I want to develop a doctrine so pure it won't have to be amended ten years from now."

Ohhhh! He's in real trouble. Flexibility of the spirit is one of the keys to happiness, health and power. Some few will stay elastic. Most will become rutted—and die, probably blaming it on the new preacher who changed the order of worship and insisted the congregation stand on the first hymn—rather than the second.

64. I Owed My Soul to the Company Store

A number of years ago I began carrying a five-dollar bill in a secret compartment in my billfold. It was my emergency money, to be used much as a person would use a spare tire in his automobile. I think I got the idea from an old friend up in South Carolina who said he never took a trip without having enough money hidden in his shoe to buy a bus ticket back home—just in case he got in a fight with his wife and she locked him out of the hotel without his credit cards.

I determined to use my spare money only on those rare occasions when there was an unexpected demand. For instance, one day in the post office I was mailing some packages when I discovered I was seventy-five cents short. Rather than gather up all my packages and fight my way back home to get the money, I just reached in my pocket and pulled out my spare tire. On another occasion I was talking with a friend at the service station while he was putting gas in his car. When he reached into his pocket, he discovered he had put in ten dollars worth, but that ten-dollar bill in his pocket was really a five-dollar bill. I was able to help him out of a very embarrassing situation.

On both occasions I replaced the five dollars as soon as possible.

A wise man once told me, "You haven't grown up until you can carry money in your pocket without spending it."

All this reminds me of an old English saying about the difference between the lords and the commoners. The commoner works for his money; the lord makes his money work for him.

It took me a number of years before I discovered the principle of making my money work for me. Most people live from paycheck to paycheck—spending all they have on things they want but don't need. Through the scheme of installment buying, they agree to pay twice for what they want to buy once—the first time to buy, the second time for the privilege of buying through interest. By the time they have paid for what they have bought, it's worn out—or broken. The wise man, on the other hand, saves, invests, sacrifices and waits until he has cash to pay.

The understanding of this spiritual principle did not come easy. For a number of years I was a slave to those little plastic idols known as credit cards. Armed in their strength, I could go anywhere, buy anything. I bought now and trusted God to pay the bills later—with interest.

Then a friend of mine, John Walters, lost his job as manager of a large supermarket. Knowing he had five children and suspecting he lived as I lived, from paycheck to paycheck, I dashed over to his house to see if he needed money.

"Oh, no," he said calmly, "we don't owe anybody anything. We don't use credit cards."

I left the house that afternoon feeling much as my brother must have felt when he visited me and learned I spoke in tongues. I was still his brother, but at the same time had become very odd. At least, I wasn't like other people. And so it was with John, for I had never met anyone—except my father—who didn't use credit cards.

That night I spent a lot of time thinking about my father. I remembered the afternoon after school when I had come into his office on 14th Avenue in Vero Beach with a new pair of shoes in a box under my arm. He asked me where I had bought them and I told him at Wodtke's Department Store across the street.

"Did you pay for them?"

"No, sir," I replied. "They said they would send us a bill at the end of the month."

"No they won't," daddy said, reaching in his pocket and pulling out a ten-dollar bill. "I'll not have any bills coming in the mail to my house. Take this and go back over there and pay for your shoes."

That was a long time ago and I had almost forgotten. Now here was another man, John Walters, who lived like that. And when he lost his job he didn't panic—because he didn't owe anyone.

Jackie and I decided that night to tear up our credit cards. The following day we informed the children. From that time on we would buy nothing except essentials until we paid off all our old debts. We also agreed that all purchases in the future would be paid in full, by cash or check. If the Lord wanted us to have a new car, we'd trust Him for the money. If He didn't we'd trust Him to heal the old one or give us peace and joy as we walked. But under no circumstances would we ever again be weighted down by monthly payments.

It took us almost a year to get out of debt—that is, until everything except the house was paid off. As we prayed about that I realized my earlier pronouncements had been radical, yet necessary to swing my pendulum back into balance. So we modified the earlier decision. I felt free to use credit cards—but only if I had money in the bank to cover the purchases, and could pay in full at the end of the month. This way I used the credit card, it didn't use me. And I would not be forced to pay interest.

Second, we realized it was wise economics—sometimes—to buy on credit an item which appreciated in cash value. Our house, for instance, was appreciating faster than we were making interest payments. A business might do the same way. On the other hand, an automobile, TV set, or vacuum cleaner depreciates in value. So on those items we would always pay cash. That was making my money work for me, rather than being a slave to my money.

The contrast of owning your money, or being owned by your debts, was pointed out very clearly when a young friend, who felt called by God to go to the mission field, came to me sorrowful. "I can't go," he said sadly. "I owe my soul to Sears Roebuck."

It is discontent, insecurity, and fear which drives men into debt. Dissatisfied with our present situation, and unwilling to live on whatever financial plateau we find ourselves, we arm billfolds with credit cards and buy today (at unbelievable interest rates) what God would give us if we only waited for His time.

The writer of Hebrews says it directly: "Be ye free from the love of money; content with such things as ye have: for himself hath said, I will in no wise fail thee, neither will I in any wise forsake thee" (Heb. 13:5 American Standard Version).

The people of God are to be free from the temptation of extravagance, luxury, and easy money because they know the God who supplies their needs. (Note: It is not faith *that* God will supply, rather faith in a God *who* supplies.)

Credit buying moves us off the mountaintop of faith and into the valley of presumption. It calls for us to cast ourselves off the pinnacle of the Temple and believe God will catch us before the bill collectors do.

Recently I was driving through Norfolk, Virginia, and pulled up at a stoplight beside a big, yellow school bus filled with nuns. Glancing out my window, I saw written on the side of the bus, "Sisters of Divine Providence."

"Wow!" I thought. "That's great. Finally there's someone who really has faith."

Then the bus pulled out in front of me, and on the back door I saw in much smaller letters, "Emergency Exit."

It seems that people of divine providence have no emergency exits. Trusting God means sealing up all the other ways out. It's like those young teenagers who said to Nebuchadnezzar, "O King, we will not serve thy gods, for our God is able to deliver us from the fiery furnace. But even if He doesn't intervene, we'll still not disobey Him."

To them, trusting God meant sealing off all emergency exits.

A number of years ago our church in Melbourne decided that all money which came into the church was to be given away that week. Nothing was to be stored away, but all was to be put to work immediately. Then we would trust God the following week to resupply all our needs.

I still believe in that principle. Money, like manna, is good only when it is used immediately. The only time we saved money was when it was specifically designated for some project down the road.

We do that in our personal lives. Saving, for the sake of saving, is faithless. We save for the children's education. We save for retirement. We save for a new car. But to save simply to save, takes God's money out of circulation and cuts off the flow of provision from the windows of Heaven.

Several years ago one of our major denominations announced they had saved enough money in a Federal Reserve Bank to support all their foreign missionaries for a full year in case of financial crisis. Now, if there had been a direct word from

THE LAST WORD

God, as there was to Joseph in Egypt, to save for the lean years, that would be a different matter. But to save just in case God let them down. . . .

Graham Kerr, the famed Galloping Gourmet, told Pat Robertson he had saved two hundred thousand dollars for a "rainy day." Pat responded that Graham must have been expecting a deluge.

There are no life preservers aboard the Good Ship Zion. Plastic credit cards may help you float a loan, but they'll never support you when you're floating alone. Only faith in Jesus Christ can do that—and that means sealing off all emergency exits.

65. Sing Me a Song

It had been a lousy day. The joy of singing "This is the day the Lord hath made" had been squeezed out of me by a hundred adverse circumstances—and four or five grouchy people. I pulled in the driveway thinking how nice it was going to be to slip off my shoes, eat a leisurely dinner, and relax with a good novel.

Jackie met me at the door. "You're late. We're supposed to be at the meeting at Mrs. Van Alstine's in thirty minutes."

I didn't want to groan out loud. I knew she'd had a busy day also. But at that stage I didn't care. I groaned anyway.

"Aw, not tonight. Someone else is leading the group. They don't need me. I'd rather stay home."

But we had promised. And a half hour later we were sitting in the luxurious living room of a fashionable home near the beach. There were about twenty people present—mostly older ladies. Everyone was stiff and formal. I wondered what they would think if I took off my shoes and slumped down in my chair.

Unlike the temptation to groan, I resisted this time. But I was miserable.

The hostess went around the room introducing each person and asking them to say a word about their various "accomplishments." I sighed. My imagination was working overtime. What if I told them I worked with pimps and prostitutes? Maybe I should tell them I was an orderly in the hospital and felt that everyone should learn to mop floors for the glory of God? Again I resisted, and when it came time for me to introduce myself I said what was expected—and they all clapped politely.

The hostess was beaming. "We're so glad you came tonight. Your lovely wife tells me you have a beautiful voice. We're all hoping you'll sing us a solo at the close of the meeting. Don't you agree, ladies?"

There was more applause. I looked around the room at the beaming faces—then I glared at Jackie. How could she put me on the spot like this?

The hostess continued. "Of course, we don't have a piano, but I know a great singer like you won't mind singing without accompaniment."

It was too much. I was horrified. I love singing, but inside there is a certain prima donna spirit which causes me to feel I should only sing under the most proper conditions: tuned piano, exceptional pianist, proper sound system, back-up musicians. To sing *a cappella* to a group of strange ladies was out of the question.

I tried every way possible to squirm out of it. I played humble. I suggested someone else. I even suggested maybe the whole group would like to sing. Nothing worked. I was stuck. "After we serve tea you can stand right over here and sing whatever you want," the hostess said as she moved on to the next person.

I was mortified. What could I do?

Sitting next to me was one of the few ladies in the room whom

I knew. She was Julia Lake Kellersberger, the saintly but enthusiastic widow of a famous Presbyterian missionary doctor. She sensed my predicament. As I sat brooding over my tea, she broke into bubbly conversation.

She began telling of her work in Africa with the lepers whose voices had been burned out by the horrible disease. They would come to church, hold their hymn books with their stubs (their hands having been eaten away by leprosy) and turn the pages with their chins. Opening their mouths they would sing praises to God. But since their vocal cords were gone, they would have to sing through silent lips.

I felt my face burning as she finished her story. Here was I, perfectly capable of singing praises to God, trying to wiggle out of it because I was too sophisticated.

At the close of the meeting I stood in the appointed place, and sang. But I had to ask the ladies to bow their heads. I didn't want them to see the tears on my face as I gave tone to the words: "How great thou art."

66. A Place for Everything

Moving into a new house assured me of one thing: I'd never have to wake up on a Saturday morning and say, "I wonder what I can find to do today." There were a million things to do—most of them scattered around on the floor.

The Saturday after we moved was Hang Pictures Day. I doubted if anyone in the entire state of Florida had as many things stored in picture frames as we did. We had certificates, diplomas, letters of recommendation, awards, commissions, locks of baby hair, needlepoint, slogans and "quaint sayings," yellowed newspaper clippings, pictures of famous people, pictures of people whose names I had forgotten, pictures of the children, pictures of me when I was thin and had hair. In fact, one reason we bought the bigger house was for more wall space.

So Saturday was time to hang pictures. Or at least to hang picture frames—some of which contained pictures.

THE LAST WORD

Things went well until we got to the framed dust jackets of my books. I wanted to put them in the front hall. Jackie suggested the utility room. We had a brief discussion accompanied by white knuckles and clenched teeth—after which we reached a compromise. I put the dust jackets in the utility room.

Next came famous persons I have worked with. I insisted my desire to hang their pictures in the front hall, most of them taken with their arm around me or my arm around them, was not egotism. No, I did not want to impress visitors, despite the fact that was the first thing they would see when they entered the house. I just liked to be reminded of my old friends . . . so I could pray for them.

Jackie nodded, and smiled. She seemed to think my prayers were much purer in the hall leading to the utility room than the front foyer.

Again, we compromised. I agreed to hang the pictures of famous persons I had known in the hall leading to the utility room.

Then she pointed to the artistically framed sheepskins. "Do hanging these diplomas on the wall make you feel educated," she asked innocently, "or just important?"

I tried to explain that a lot of people wanted to know where I went to college, what seminary I graduated from, what kind of degrees I had earned. Hanging those sheepskins in the front hall would answer all the questions before they were asked. Actually, it was a service to our guests.

"I think you ought to hang them behind the bookcase in your study," she said. "That way, if you are ever studying away and wonder if you're really stupid or that's just a lie from Satan, you can get up and read your diplomas and know you are actually a very smart person."

I felt like the man who had received a button for being humble—and then had it taken away because he wore it.

I guess it all depends on my depth of security. Is it "in Christ"?

Is my BA (Born Again) degree really all I need? If so, why all this stuff in frames?

So, we compromised. The diplomas are in a trunk in the attic. And Corrie ten Boom, Kathryn Kuhlman and Pat Robertson smile at us back near the washing machine. And in case you wonder where I hung my old high school National Honor Society certificate, well, you'll see it when you pull into the garage—hanging over the workbench.

67. The World is Watching

The young poet from Scotland was trying to force himself to listen to the dull sermon. Instead of looking at the preacher, though, his eyes wandered to the back of the hat of the woman in front of him. Bobby Burns was fascinated by the presence of a tiny louse crawling around on it. As a result he wrote his own sermon that day:

> O wad some Power the giftie gie us
> To see oursels as others see us.

Now it seems that we may have been given just such a power. It is called television.

For several months, on a monthly basis, I had been flying to Charlotte, North Carolina, to appear as a guest, and sometimes host, on the Christian interview show—The PTL Club. The two-hour program is shown live in the Charlotte area and videotaped to be played on several hundred stations across the nation.

Then came the big moment—I was going to actually see myself on our home TV screen. The program was going to be beamed into our small Florida community via cable TV.

It was a devastating experience.

Our entire family and a couple of friends crowded into our den to eagerly watch the program. But when my weird face appeared on the screen, instead of applauding everyone began to giggle.

"Why do you keep sticking your finger in your ear?" our thirteen-year-old Sandy laughed hysterically.

"And look at the way you bat your eyes a hundred times a minute," my wife commented between gales of laughter.

"Why do you keep looking out of the sides of your eyes?" Tim asked.

That one I could explain. Host Jim Bakker, who was off camera at the time, had knocked over his water glass. While my mouth was talking to the camera, my eyes were watching Jim mop up the mess on the table. To the viewers it left a weird impression.

There were a lot of other things I noticed. For some odd reason, when I finish talking and relax, my head begins to lean over to one side. One time it leaned so far my ear touched my shoulder. It looked like I was deformed.

I hunkered down in my chair in the den and hoped the picture tube would blow out before we got to the part where I tried to stand up and snagged my coat pocket on the microphone.

But it was all there. Captured faithfully on videotape. Coat, microphone, loud screeching noise and all. After the gales of laughter in our den had died down, I noticed that when I sat back down (after having almost ripped the microphone off the stand), my leisure jacket had scrunched up around the back of my neck. Nobody in the studio told me, so for the rest of the program I sat there with my coat collar up around the top of my head, giving the camera one of my stupid grins, and batting my eyes a hundred times a minute.

Surely things will get better, I told myself. But that day, after appearing before seventy-five million people with my finger in my ear and my neck bent sideways, I had a bit of a problem with the power to see myself as everyone else does.

Harold Hill told me that praise and thanksgiving were the answer to all my problems. Well, I don't know about that. I'll leave it up to the experts. But I now have something to be really happy about—we've moved out in the country and don't have cable TV. I'm glad others can see me. I'm gladder I can't see myself.

68. Who Turned the Pressure Up?

Several years ago I installed an underground sprinkling system in our yard. Contrary to California propaganda, it does not rain all the time in Florida. But without water the grass dies, and a sprinkling system seemed the way out.

Unfortunately, plumbers in our town are rarely available. They have a busy schedule racing sports cars and flying to Acapulco. I was stuck with installing the sprinkling system myself.

With the help of my children, I finally managed to dig up the yard, lay what seemed to be endless miles of PVC pipe, then, using an abundance of tape, glue and clamps, got the thing hooked up. Like repairing a locomotive that is roaring down the tracks, the job was technically interesting but not much fun.

A friend gave me a rebuilt three-quarter-horsepower pump which I hooked to a pipe that ran into the lake in our back yard. Presto, we had water on the lawn.

But something was wrong. The water was not evenly distributed and unless we had a strong east wind, a portion of the yard never got wet. Besides, the pump kept breaking down.

After three years of fiddling with the thing, I went out and bought a brand new two-horsepower pump. I spent most of a Monday running a larger intake pipe out into the lake and installing the new pump. Then came the moment of truth as I stepped inside the back door and flipped the switch. The pump whirred into life and we had water. I mean, we really had water.

Where my old system, held together with glue, rotting tape, and rusty clamps, had been sufficient for the three-quarter-horsepower pump, it was totally inadequate for the big new pump which exerted more than twice the pressure. Water squirted everywhere. Underground connections burst loose and erupted in the yard like geysers, blowing dirt and grass up with them. Tape peeled off exposed connections, sending out streams of water. Tiny pinholes in the pipes, unnoticed before, suddenly opened to spray water in all directions. Loose sprinkler heads were thrown high into the air as water roared upward in gushers. Flaws, blemishes, and defects which had remained unnoticed were suddenly exposed as the new power surged through.

I guess I should have expected something like that, for the same thing had happened to me several years before. I had sputtered along on low spiritual power for almost twenty years, when suddenly I was filled with a new power—the Holy Spirit. Talk about leak, I looked like a sieve.

I remember someone once asked Bob Mumford what was the evidence of the baptism in the Holy Spirit. He answered in one word: "Problems."

Charismatics and others who take themselves too seriously often give the impression that once a person receives the Holy Spirit all his problems are solved. From that time on, the fantasy goes, the Christian moves from mountaintop to mountaintop.

Well, that's partially true, but what they fail to point out is the way you get from one mountaintop to another is to crawl through a valley.

I was shocked, after receiving the baptism in the Holy Spirit, to find I was capable of violently losing my temper, was afflicted with lust, and occasionally was even tempted to renounce my faith. Now I understand that the surge of power was exposing my defects and flaws, causing me to leak all over the place—often in front of everyone. (That, I later discovered, was God's method of teaching me patience and humility.)

I am sure my leaking caused many of my friends to say, "If that's the way Spirit-filled people act, I don't want any of it." That's too bad, and I am sorry I made such a mess, but it seems to be the only way God could get me to see my flaws. And for the first time in my life I began to look at my defects not as problems, but as challenges.

Six months after she received the fullness of the Spirit, a young housewife confessed she was back in the valley of depression. In a moment of weakness she gave way to an old temptation. By the time I saw her she had convinced herself there was no hope. She was doomed to the valley. Much of her self-condemnation, she later revealed (after she had reappeared on the mountaintop with a new understanding of forgiveness), had come from those who shared only the victories of the Spirit-walk, rather than the constant struggle of being knocked down and letting God pick you up.

There is a constant temptation to gloss over the defects and failures—recounting only the victories. But the walk in the Spirit is a balance of falling downs and getting ups, darkness and light, valleys and mountaintops, sins and saintliness, defeats and victories. Every life and every ministry is full of leaks. Credibility can only be achieved when we tell it like it really is. Leaks and all.

69. Is There Electricity in Heaven?

Whoever writes those "assembly and installation" instructions for the electrical fixtures needs to be exposed for what he is. An agent from the pit.

Unfortunately, my method of punishing such people is no longer considered humane. I suggest all people who write these unintelligible instructions be afforded the same punishment they used to give a person caught spreading gossip. Put an iron collar around his neck and chain him to the front steps of the courthouse. Everyone who walks by is then encouraged to spit on him.

For five years the ceiling light in our kitchen has been broken. Once every three months my wife hits her head on the corner of one of the cabinets in the darkened room and comes roaring into the den where I am sitting with a magazine. Shaking her bloody fist, which she has been using to hold her head, she threatens, "If you can't get me a new light you can just fix your own supper from now on." I kiss her wounds, say soothing words and promise to do it "as soon as I have time," which is the same as saying "we'll see" when one of the children asks if he can use the family station wagon in the Saturday night drag races.

However, last Sunday afternoon I finally had a few minutes and decided to do my wife a favor. I had bought one of those fluorescent fixtures with the circular bulbs. The instructions, written by someone on LSD, were impossible to follow.

"If your fixture has a yellow, white and purple label on the advance ballast. . . ."

I didn't even know whether my fixture had a ballast, much less an advance ballast—whatever those things are. So I just did the best I could, spreading everything out on the kitchen floor and trying to keep from screaming while I struggled with the instructions.

It was hopeless. I finally went completely out of control when I got down to instruction 12 which read: "Thread two screws (3) into crossbar (2) all the way, and attach crossbar (2) to the outlet box with two outlet box screws (4)." Under this was something which said, "NOTE: outlet box screws (4) are supplied with your outlet box."

What the writer of those instructions didn't seem to realize was my outlet box was coated with grease, dust, five coats of paint and some dried blood—and hadn't seen a screw in five years.

Now what do you do? It's Sunday afternoon, time for church, the power is off in half the house, screws and junk are spread all over the cabinet and floor, and a whole gang of kids are coming over any minute for supper.

I did what any sensible person would have done. I blew up. I smashed something against the floor which bounced high off the wall and rolled into the den. Then I straightened up and smashed the corner of my bald head on the corner of the kitchen cabinet.

I kept hoping, hoping, hoping I would hear someone in the next room laughing. That would give me all the excuse I needed to grab the entire light fixture and hurl it with exceeding force at the wall. But God's grace was sufficient. All was silent. Even my wife held her tongue and wisely said nothing—waiting for the storm to pass.

I finally got the light in place, thanks to some clothesline wire and a huge screw the size of a coal chisel which I forced up through a jagged hole in the ceiling. Jackie cleaned up the debris and blood while I took delight in not following the last instruction which said, "File this sheet for future reference."

My friends tell me that if I do not forgive my enemies, God will not forgive me. I am having a difficult time, especially with the person who writes instructions for installation. But I'll give it a try. One thing is sure. Next time I'll call an electrician. No light fixture is worth losing your place in Heaven.

70. My Friend the Door

The former owner of our house was a wood-carving enthusiast. When he moved out, he left behind six handsome, carved redwood shutters on the front windows, and a splendid hand-carved front door. The door is a relief carving of twining grapevines from which hang big bunches of luscious grapes. On top, on either side of the one-way glass mirror which serves as a window, are two beautiful birds of paradise. Unlike other front doors, it has personality. Across the years it became a good friend who welcomed me home from all parts of the world.

However, the years had not been kind to the door. The untreated redwood had warped and big cracks had opened along the seams. The weather had discolored it and when it rained, it swelled up so tight it was impossible to open and close. It seemed I had no choice but to take it down and replace it with a factory-made door.

But the door had other friends besides me. Led by my own

children, neighborhood kids began coming by the house saying, "Please don't take it down. It's the most beautiful door in all the world."

But I didn't see how it could be saved. Despite the fact it was a dear old friend who had faithfully protected my family while I was gone and welcomed me home from many ports of call, it was seemingly beyond repair. Like a heartbroken cowboy who is forced to shoot his lame horse, I had no choice but to replace it.

Last Friday I purchased a new, factory-made, solid core door from the building supply company. "I know it is plain," I told my children who met me with disappointed looks, "but maybe we can decorate it with paint."

I put on some old clothes and got to work unscrewing hinges. Minutes later the front yard was filled with children from all over the neighborhood, who along with my own kids were chanting something that sounded like "Woodman, spare that door." I felt like Jack the Ripper in a carpenter's apron.

"Okay, I'll try," I said. "But I think it's hopeless."

The rest of the day was spent opening seams, wirebrushing and steelwooling vines, grapes, and birds, applying sealer, gluing panels, drilling dowel holes, caulking the window, and finally clamping the door back together. It was almost midnight when I finally finished, but it looked like I had, indeed, saved the door.

I bedded it down in the den overnight and hung plastic sheeting over the front opening. The next morning the neighborhood kids gathered to watch me rehang their old friend. Despite the fact the mirror has a big crack down the middle, it really looks good. And the building supply people cheerfully refunded my money.

Yesterday evening I stood out in the front yard just at dusk. The setting sun reflected off the redwood relief carvings, setting the grapes and vines forth in shadowed splendor. A deep feeling of satisfaction welled up inside me. I had saved the door.

"Thanks, friend," I could almost hear it say. "I'll do my best to shield you from the enemy and welcome your friends."

I gave it an affectionate pat as I went inside. What more could I ask from an old friend?

71. Better to Be Kind Than to Be Right

I had just finished speaking to a large group in the Atlanta Civic Auditorium. The subject was "Restoration—the Fresh Move of God's Spirit Today."

Still flushed with the excitement of ministering under God's anointing, I stepped off the stage to speak to the usual flock of well-wishers.

"Thank you . . . yes, God is good . . . yes, I remember you from Cincinnati . . . it's nice to know your husband reads *Logos Journal* . . . so glad to see you again . . . sorry, I don't have time to read your four-hundred-page manuscript before dinner. . . ."

Suddenly I was looking into the narrowed eyes of a very intense man. His lips were pursed and grayish in color. His Bible was open to Peter's warning about false teachers.

"You almost told these people to come out of their dead denominational churches," he said in a thin voice.

"You're right," I answered. "I *almost* did. But I didn't."

He pointed his finger at the Bible. "But why didn't you tell them the denominational church is Babylon? They need to be warned before it is too late."

I suspected I was about to waste my breath, but I could not let the question go begging.

"I'll tell you why," I said. "For the same reason King David refused to take action against King Saul, even though Saul had turned his back on God. David knew it was God who set Saul in his position; and it was God who would have to remove him. Besides, Saul gave David his start in the ministry. When Saul turned apostate, David's soldiers wanted to take his life. David prevented it. 'For who can stretch forth his hand against the Lord's anointed, and be guiltless?' "

As I suspected, the man didn't hear me. He walked away, muttering something about preachers who had lost their salt. But the principle remains valid. God will not hold us guiltless if we take up the sword against His anointed—even if they are attempting to kill us.

There is enough division in the Body already without me or anyone else trying to knock down somebody else's straw horse.

If a man does not agree with my doctrine, that is his problem, not mine. Like Nehemiah, why should I come down from the task God has given me, to debate silly questions? Instead of proving him wrong I should love him, pray for him, encourage him where he is right and forgive him where he is ignorant.

My old Pentecostal friend, David du Plessis, puts it this way: "God has not called me to accuse the brethren. He has called me to forgive."

A wise man once told me, "To be right satisfies the ego. To be kind satisfies God." And in the flyleaf of my Bible I have written, "Jamie, you cannot defend the Holy Spirit and reveal Him at the same time."

It is time to focus on the things that unite us, rather than the things that divide. This means I cannot stretch forth my hand against the Lord's anointed lest haply I be found even to fight against God. Whether my enemies return that grace is irrevelant. I have no choice but to return love for evil done.

72. *Out Behind the Barn*

Someplace between the ages of seven and seventeen most boys (and girls?) have their first try at smoking. Like drinking beer, no one ever seems to like it to begin with. Yet because of some warped sense of manhood, many keep puffing away until they finally overcome the natural dislike and become addicted.

No one can deny that smoking is a fascinating thing. No one in my family ever smoked. My mother never allowed anybody to smoke in our house. One of the familiar sights of childhood was seeing some of my father's very distinguished guests having to walk far out into the grove behind the house to puff on his weed, while mother stood resolutely at the door to make sure he didn't come back into the house until he had exhaled every last molecule. In fact, I remember being punished one time for bringing home an empty cigar box to keep my marbles in. As a result, by the time I was twelve I had an insatiable urge to try smoking.

THE LAST WORD

A young blond-headed buddy of mine suggested I should start with rabbit tobacco. It seems he had smoked rabbit tobacco up on his aunt's farm in Georgia and it was just the thing. It never occurred to me that rabbit tobacco was some kind of weed, so I went out into the palmetto patch beside our house, found what I thought was rabbit tobacco, rolled it into some kind of cigarette, and smoked it. It was horrible, and I later told my friend what I thought of his suggestion. He finally stopped laughing long enough to explain that I had been smoking rabbit manure.

Yet even this didn't dissuade me from one day getting hold of the real thing. By the time I was fifteen I had smoked everything from grapevines to coffee (the latter smoked in a homemade pipe). I had burned my tongue, scorched my throat, almost set the grove on fire and burned a huge hole in a new pair of pants. Yet I kept at it.

My big day came when I marched into a local drug store and bought two plastic-tipped cigars. Cigarettes didn't seem manly enough, I guess, so I started with cigars. I went home that evening after football practice, walked far back into the grove behind the house, leaned against a palm tree, and became a man. (Even today, I still recommend rabbit manure over cigars.)

By the time I had finished the second one I was in horrible shape. Full of manhood, I staggered back toward the house. As I approached the back door, I realized I was reeking. One of my football coaches smoked cigars, and you could smell him all the way across the campus. I knew I was even worse. Also I knew of my mother's nose for nicotine. I slipped into the house, rummaged through the kitchen cabinets, found a handful of cloves, and dumped them into my mouth. Now if smoking leaves isn't bad enough, chewing cloves finished it off. By the time I got up off my knees in the bathroom (and I wasn't praying either—unless it was to live through the ordeal), I vowed I'd never smoke another cigar. And I haven't.

Then last week I was getting out of a taxi at National Airport in

Washington, D.C., and found a fifty-cent cigar on the seat. For some unexplained reason I stuck it in my pocket and brought it home, and hid it in my desk. It didn't stay hidden. Yesterday I stepped out in the back yard and heard the scurrying of feet, accompanied by loud coughing and giggling. I looked around the corner of the house and there stood my two boys, ages twelve and seventeen, each smoking half of that cigar.

"Go to it," I told them. "Puff it good." They were startled, but pleased and started puffing away.

"Now you can't come into the house smelling like that," I told them as they started to turn green. "But if you'll chew on these cloves perhaps your mother won't notice the smell on your breath."

I doubt seriously if either of them ever becomes a cigar smoker.

73. A Two-Hundred-Pound Watermelon

After thirty-nine years of living around oceans, lakes, and rivers, I finally got "up" on a pair of water skis.

No, I didn't make it up the first time. In fact, after the first effort I didn't think I would even make it up to the surface.

"I've tried before," I told my friend O.K. Owens, who insisted his 120-horsepower boat could pull me. "I always wind up going straight to the bottom."

O.K. flashed his Billy Graham smile and said, "Trust the Lord, brother, and just hang on."

I stood on the shore and watched as he pulled his four kids, two at a time, around the lagoon. They all looked like miniature Dick Popes. I watched them, even his eight-year-old, gliding easily behind the maroon boat, leaping across the wake, waving at the folks on the bank. "If those kids can do it, so can I," I determined.

At last I was ready. My skis in place, I leaned back on my life jacket in the briny water. Tips up. Straight ahead. Green nylon rope floating between the ski tips, the rod grasped tightly in both hands. Ahead of me the powerful boat rocked gently on the waves.

"Go!" I shouted.

The rope tightened and I held on desperately. For a fleeting moment I thought my arms were going to separate from my body in the vicinity of my shoulders. But I kept remembering those little kids and hung on.

I knew if I leaned forward I'd never get my skis back under me. I leaned back, still in my crouched position. The boat was gaining speed, but I was sinking, crouched like a ball, my skis up and ahead of me. Dimly, beyond the roar of the water around my ears, I could hear people shouting. But I had no time to listen. I had the ridiculous picture in my mind of a watermelon on a rope being pulled along behind a speeding boat. My head was all the way under now and the water was being flushed up my nose in great amounts, coming out, I assume, through my ears. But I was determined not to let go, even if I drowned or, more horrible, was scraped across a submerged oyster bar.

Suddenly the pressure slacked. The boat stopped. I bobbed to the surface and even before I could see, I could hear the gales of hysterical laughter from the shore.

"You forgot to stand up," O.K. shouted from the bobbing boat. "Try again," I gurgled back.

This time, by herculean effort, I rose to my feet. "Praise the Lord," I shouted and promptly fell forward on my face.

On the third try I made it up to stay. "Not bad for a 200-pound beginner," I thought as I circled the lagoon. Every muscle in my body ached as I struggled to keep the skis under me, but it made no difference. I had achieved another of my life's goals.

My eleven-year-old Timmy was next in line. "Remember, daddy's a lot stronger than you," I told him as I handed him the rope. "Don't be discouraged if you don't get up today. We can always come back later."

The motor roared, the rope tightened, and Timmy glided to his feet, following the speeding boat around the river. On his second trip around he leaped the wake, waved at the crowd, and grinned. I waded back to shore and collapsed, exhausted, on the grass. He made it look so easy. But why not? Look at the example I had set for him.

74. Anything to Keep From Writing

For some odd reason, most writers detest the task of answering their mail. Mine collects in a huge pile beside my typewriter. Sometimes it doesn't even get opened. There it lays for days and weeks, moldering and turning yellow around the edges. Finally my conscience begins to scream so loud I can't hear anything else, and gritting my teeth I go into my studio, close the door, and by a sheer act of my will bang out letters.

With three children in college, I try to keep in touch with them on a weekly basis. But even there I find myself falling behind, finding it much easier to pick up the phone late at night and call. Anything to keep from writing.

A newspaper columnist loves to sit down at his typewriter and bang out opinions on various subjects. Reporters enjoy snooping through the news and coming up with a written story. Book writers live for the time when they can put pen to paper and let the words flow, describing characters, creating suspense, and painting descriptive scenes of places and events. But let these same people come face to face with a huge stack of mail, all of it clamoring for a personal answer, and they go paranoid.

Movie actors are the same way. A man may be Mister Perfect in his relationship with his screen partner. But after the day at the studio is over, he goes home and shouts at his wife, refuses to communicate, and sleeps on the sofa.

One of my best friends is a medical doctor. If I visit him in his office, he is careful to prescribe just what I should eat and how I should treat my body. But when we go out to lunch together, he orders roast pork, french fried potatoes, dessert with gobs of whipped cream, five cups of coffee with white sugar, and smokes half a pack of cigarettes.

Another of my friends is a construction engineer. He spends his days building houses—following blueprints perfectly. But the closet door his wife has been trying to get him to hang still leans against the wall of his bedroom where it has been for two years.

Sadly, the same rule sometimes applies to the professional Christian. Pay a man to minister and he does a good job from nine to five but after hours things sometimes get slack.

Some things are meant to be more than jobs. They are life styles. I guess answering my mail ought to fall into that category. And so should my devotion to God—no matter how much I might want to chuck the whole thing sometimes.

75. My Old Friend

Occasionally I will break away from my family and retire to a small cabin in the mountains of North Carolina to work on a book manuscript. I love the mountains—and I love the solitude. But there is something about that place in particular which makes me want to call every mountain man I meet Kenneth Summey.

Now it's not that Kenneth Summey is not a good name. It's a fine name. An honorable name. In fact it is the name of a childhood friend I used to know in North Carolina, a boy who lived right across the ridge from that same cabin who used to come over and "mess around" with me when our family would come up for our annual summer vacation. Ever since then I've wanted to see Kenneth again. The trouble is nobody around there seems to be named that any more.

It's been more than thirty years since I saw Kenneth Summey. I remember him as a red-headed, freckle-faced, bare-footed son of a mountain farmer. During the summer we would roam the woods together, throw rocks at rabbits and do some talking. In the fall I would return to school in Florida and he would stay on with his mountain family. That was thirty years ago and I never think of him now. That is, until I get up to the mountains and some strange man knocks on the door of the cabin, at which time I go rushing out, exclaiming, "Well, well, Kenneth Summey."

I did that last summer in front of my entire family. Mr. Osteen, whose children come across the chigger trail and play with our children when we spend a few weeks at the cabin in the summer, had knocked on the door one evening to tell his two little girls to come home. I came bursting out on the porch saying, "Well, if it isn't Kenneth Summey."

Of course, it wasn't. It was Herbert Osteen. But he was too shy to correct me and let me stand there talking to "good old Kenneth" before finally motioning inside for his children to come home with him. I kept wondering why Kenneth would be coming after the Osteen kids.

My children thought I had fallen out of my tree. They all knew Mr. Osteen and had never even heard of Kenneth Summey, who belongs to my childhood, not theirs. Mr. Osteen later told my embarrassed children not to feel bad. A lot of nuts from Florida visit North Carolina in the summer.

The next week I was working on the stone wall along the driveway which goes down to the paved road when a car pulled up and stopped. The man at the wheel leaned over and called my name. I wiped sweat from my eyes and, before I could stop myself, said, "Well, well, Kenneth Summey."

Of course, it wasn't. It was Jim Ballard, pastor of the Baptist church in town. I cleared my throat, made some apology about the sun and sweat and hoped he hadn't heard what I called him—knowing full well he had.

Then the following summer, when I was at the cabin for a

two-week stretch by myself, finishing up a book, it happened again. I was feeding the ponies in the side pasture when I saw a red-headed man coming up the drive. There was no doubt about it. I hollered out, "Good old Kenneth." But it wasn't, of course. It never is. It was Wade Thompson, another Baptist preacher.

I don't know what's wrong with me. I wonder what would happen if the real Kenneth Summey were to show up. I'd probably grab his hand and call him Jamie Buckingham.

After that last incident I came back into the cabin and took a hot tub bath, wishing my wife and family would hurry up and join me in the mountains. They have a way, even if it is by laughing at me, of easing the pain of my blunders. Of course as soon as I got settled in the tub the garbage man was pounding at the door, wanting to know if anyone was home and if they were, did they have any garbage to be collected. (Garbage men in the mountains do things a bit different than we do in the flatlands.) I didn't know whether to get up or sit tight. I opted for sitting tight, fearing my appearance at the door would be too much of a shock for the poor fellow.

Besides, it just might have been Kenneth Summey. And I would hate for him to see me, after all these years, standing at the door stark naked, hand extended, calling him Jamie Buckingham.

76. *Not Even a Little Backbiting, Lord?*

As the car far down the road in front of me sped past the hitchhiker without stopping, the young man alongside the road exchanged his thumb for a middle finger and made an obscene gesture at the departing car. Then, seeing me coming, he turned, grinned, and stuck out his thumb.

Had I even considered picking him up earlier, I forgot about it when he vented his anger at the earlier car.

Shooting birds at passing cars never gets anyone a ride. And shooting holes in the Good Ship Zion, regardless of how slow she is sailing or how badly off course she seems to be, never leads anyone into the light.

When I feel like punishing myself, I sit back and remember the details of that Friday afternoon in Wilson, North Carolina. Jackie and I were visiting with our friends, Allen and Irene Harrell. Judge Harrell took me around to meet the local Methodist minister. I enjoyed chatting with him in his study until he asked me about my ministry. Then I saddled my favorite horse and rode roughshod over him and the institution he represented, vociferously condemning all the "dead churches." He listened patiently to my tirade and finally said, "Could it be, brother, that we are not dead, only ignorant, waiting for someone to show us the light?"

What a gentle rebuke. Yet even to this day I realize I was not a lamplighter, but a candlesnuffer.

I have a letter in my files from Mrs. Billy Graham. Ruth had read the first draft of one of my first books in which I had a chapter exposing the fallacies of a certain Pentecostal organization. She wrote: "There are enough worldlings shooting holes in the church without us joining the firing squad. Billy and I often remind ourselves of Saul's disagreement with David. Yet it was David who said of Saul's defeat, 'Tell it not in Gath, publish it not in the streets of Askelon; lest the daughters of the Philistines rejoice' " (2 Samuel 1:20).

Peter Lord, one of my favorite Baptist pastors, sometimes chides me with a gentle rebuke, saying, "Don't be so rough on the brethren, Jamie. Just love us."

There is no place in the Body of Christ for a backbiter. (A backbiter is a backstabber who has misplaced his knife.) The Body is made up of ALL who call Jesus Lord. That includes those who believe in miracles and those who don't. It includes opposites like John R. Rice and Pope Paul VI, Billy Graham and Bob Jones, Norman Vincent Peale and Morris Cerullo, Bob Mumford and Pat Robertson, Jerome Hines and the Cameron Family Singers.

These and millions of other disagreeing saints make up the Body. As members of this family we are commanded by our Father not to backbite, criticize, accuse, or condemn. If we have a difference we are to go to one another in person. Only if a man is making public pronouncements do we have the right to publicly rebuke him. And even then, it must be in love.

If those who claim to be filled with the Spirit will love all those who say it is impossible, and if those who believe in miracles will exhibit the greatest miracle of all, the miracle of love, then one day we'll wake up and find we're one in the Spirit. And they'll know we are Christians by our love.

77. A Sure Way to Get Stoned

One of my unfulfilled desires is to write a column that will please everyone. Common sense, however, tells me it will never be done.

Besides the columns I have written for various Christian magazines, I also write a weekly editorial page column for my hometown newspaper. I try to keep things as bland as possible, but invariably I stir up some reader who retaliates with smoking pen or threatening call. More often than not it's my adjectives which rub people the wrong way, rather than my verbs. Adjectives have a way of doing that, and words like chubby, gingham-clad, balding, and ignorant have a way of bringing out the true nature of my readers.

I remember a column I wrote about my cousin Henry who was a Presbyterian pastor before he went into marriage counseling. His family visited us one time and his son's pet corn snake—a six-foot yellow serpent—escaped in the house. Four days after he left, my screaming wife found it under one of the children's beds. We finally got it in a box and turned it loose behind the local Presbyterian church—which seemed like poetic justice. Every Presbyterian in a sixty-mile radius was angry with me for that.

Another time I observed that most church music was more dead than alive. I suggested a few folks ought to go out and buy a tambourine and take it to church next Sunday to liven things up. After all, if they have harps in Heaven, it seemed folks ought to be getting ready down here with a little joy. This time the Baptists, Methodists, Episcopalians, and a lot of other breeds I didn't even know existed called the editor and said the Presbyterians, for once, had been right. I should be fired as a columnist. It had the distinct odor of tar and feathers being warmed over the fire.

Fortunately, the Catholics, Pentecostals, Nazarenes, and a little group who met in a tent outside of town came to my defense and I was allowed to keep on writing. Strange bedfellows.

Then a year or so ago I visited a small town in Appalachia and wrote my observations in a column. The column was plucked from the local paper by a retired resident of that community and sent northward, where it was reprinted as an example of the way flatland touristers think of mountain folk. It caused great wrath on the part of the readers in Appalachia because I had intimated some of the people in that location were prone to violence. One man wrote me a fiery letter and said the people in his region were not at all violent—and if I didn't retract my statement, someone just might come down to Florida and burn my house down. I called the out-of-state editor to see what I could do to smooth things over. He told me not to worry. Sure, some of the people were angry and had on occasion shot people they disagreed with, but on the whole they were peace-loving.

It brought to mind a reported incident that took place when I was a boy in Florida. The story had it that a writer from *Sports Illustrated* came south from New York to write a story on frog-gigging in the little sugar cane community of Fellsmere. In his article he also described Saturday nights in Fellsmere—complete with shootings, stabbings, and drunken brawls. His reporting so infuriated the citizens, who said they weren't at all like that, that they took up a collection from the sugar cane workers, bought a round-trip train ticket to New York, and sent their brawlingest frog-gigger to New York for the express purpose of seeking out the Yankee writer and beating him up.

Last year I wrote what I thought was a humorous column of my experience of going out to buy a new car. I was convinced that every car salesman I talked to was trying to take advantage of me, and couldn't help but laugh when, in the process of telling me what a great car he had, one salesman opened the trunk and had the entire lid come off in his hand.

Well, the car dealers in my hometown didn't think that was very funny. They called the editor and threatened to drop all their advertising unless I ran a retraction of my innuendos in the next edition of the paper.

So I wrote another column in which I said I did not mean to imply that ALL car salesmen were liars and cheats, any more than I intended to imply that all lawyers were shysters and all preachers hypocrites.

This time the editor called me and suggested we just drop the whole incident. Not only had he lost the automobile advertising and the church page, but the car dealers and the ministers had gotten with the lawyers and were threatening to sue him.

Now you can see why I want to write something—sometime—which will please everyone. But the field is limited. Even motherhood, with the pro-abortionists and women's libbers ranting around the country, is no longer popular. And apple pie? Well, maybe you haven't been in a health food store recently, but there's a big movement abroad in America to scratch the entire phrase, "as American as apple pie" and substitute "yogurt" or "wheat grass" instead. And you'll never believe what the nutritionists are suggesting you do with your cup of coffee. Not in a hundred years—without sugar and cream, too.

Someone said Jesus came to comfort the afflicted and afflict the comfortable. I'm not in His league yet—although I'm certainly on His side. But I think I'm beginning to understand what He had to contend with in His effort to communicate—and stay alive at the same time.

78. You Don't Need to Spike the Eggnog

Despite the fact that all famous gourmet chefs in the world are men, there seems to be something unnatural about a man in the kitchen. When the people of Israel asked Samuel for a king, Samuel replied that the forthcoming king would set the people in proper order. Their sons would be soldiers and their daughters would be "confectionaries, cooks, and bakers."

I should have remembered that when I got my last annual urge to cook something in the kitchen. As a cook I make a pretty good soldier. It was during that time between Thanksgiving and Christmas when I began to get a desire to drink eggnog. Unfortunately, the craving to cook and the craving for eggnog arrived almost simultaneously. When I announced to Jackie what I intended to do, she sighed and said she was taking the children down to see their grandparents.

"I'll be back and clean up your mess later," she said.

The Better Homes and Gardens Cookbook recipe

called for two egg yolks mixed with sugar and then mixed with four cups of milk. This was to be warmed over medium heat until the mixture "covered the spoon." Already I was in trouble. The mixture covered the spoon the instant I stuck the spoon in the bowl. I assumed that "cover the spoon" was a technical term understood by eggnog-makers, but it left me cold. I began to suspect I was in for a long afternoon.

I forged ahead, heating the mixture in a saucepan. It tasted good. In fact, it tasted so good I decided to double the recipe. That was my second mistake. Don't ever add egg yolks to anything hot. They do something strange. The brew was beginning to look like something you'd order in a Chinese restaurant along with your egg rolls.

With all that egg floating around on top of the nog, I quickly decided to strain some of it off. That was another mistake. The only thing I could find in the kitchen bigger than a tea strainer to strain off the scrambled eggs on top of the nog was a colander. Colanders, I discovered after I began pouring the mixture, not only strain up and down—they strain sideways. A good bit of the eggnog wound up on the floor—much to the delight of the cat. Again I doubled the recipe to make up for the overflow.

The next step was to beat the egg whites in the electric mixer until fluffy and then "fold in" to the other stuff. I sensed that "fold in" was another technical term which was going to give me trouble. But I didn't have to worry about it because I never could get the egg whites to do what they were supposed to do—that is, stand up in little peaks like the meringue on those lemon pies you see in cafeterias. All they did was swish around in the bottom of the bowl with the sugar I kept adding.

I needed something in a hurry to make them stiff so I could "fold them into" the now boiling mixture on the stove. First I added a little cornstarch but all that did was make huge lumps. Then I found some "whipping cream" in the refrigerator. I added it and turned the mixer speed to "fast." All it did was swish around in the bottom of the bowl and then swish out all over the floor.

By this time I had added another two quarts of milk to the liquid on the stove and doubled the number of eggs to make up for those I had strained out earlier. By now I had used up all the available pots and pans and was forced to shift to the bottom of Jackie's roaster. This, combined with the old double boiler which I found in the bathroom while looking for burn ointment, gave me almost enough containers to hold the seething, bubbling mixture which seemed to expand rapidly under heat.

Approximately one hour, two broken eggs, and one scalded cat later, I was ready to "fold in" the lumpy mess in the mixer bowl. However, it was obvious that the addition of that mixture to the mixture which already came to the brim of the roaster bottom, the two double boiler pans, and the big saucepan, would cause a massive overflow. I ran back to the bathroom for adhesive tape. Taping the steam hole in the roaster pan top closed, I turned it upside down and put it on the open oven door—since all the burners on the stove were occupied full time. After carefully pouring from one pan to another, I was able to get most of the nog equally divided and then "folded in" the swishing egg whites.

The recipe said to add nutmeg and vanilla "to taste," which was obviously another technical term. Since I like both, I added a good bit.

I have heard you can get stoned on nutmeg. The same is true with vanilla extract. And since no one in our family drinks, it seemed that this was just the right addition to the eggnog to give it that holiday spirit.

Unfortunately, instead of two quarts I had to bottle a little more than two and a half gallons of the stuff. Even though I'm the only one who drinks it, once you shake it up, break the crust on top, and strain out the lumps with your teeth, it's not too bad.

Jackie came home and muttered something about the

THE LAST WORD

plagues of Egypt where the frogs got in the ovens. But I was rather proud of myself. It's been three weeks and the eggnog seems to be getting better with age. That's fortunate, for it looks like it's going to be around the house for a long time.

79. Will the Real You Please Stand Up?

The average man lives behind a mask. His smiles, his laughter, his piousness, his confidence are all part of the role he is playing. Seldom, if ever, does he let anyone know who he really is. Only in times of pain, fear, or perhaps when he is drinking does his mask come down and we see him as he really is.

When a man is terrified, he forgets about winning friends and influencing people. Men stride into their businesses each morning with an air of supremacy. They sit at a bar and laugh uproariously. Or, they let sage advice fall from their pseudo-intellectual lips. But they never let anyone know that behind their wisecracks and supposed indifference, they are lonely, scared and hurting. However, let that man be exposed to pain or fear and suddenly he drops his mask and flees—revealing for all the world to see who he really is.

For thirty-five years I was involved in mask-wearing.

Dissatisfied with myself, I was continually imitating someone who seemed successful—never dreaming that he, too, was probably wearing a mask. I dreaded the thought that one day someone might peek behind it, see the real me, and reject me as a person. In fact, one of my recurring nightmares was that one Sunday morning some stranger would walk into our million-dollar sanctuary, come to the front, point his finger at me and scream, "FRAUD!" And I knew I had no answer.

Then I had a life-changing experience with the Holy Spirit—and everything seemed different. Once afraid of growing bald, I had even considered a mask for the top of my head. Then came a new freedom to grow bald for the glory of God.

A middle-aged minister stopped by the house one night, his face gray and his eyes dark from fatigue. "Even after twenty years in the ministry," he said, "I still have times of doubt and depression. I am afraid to expose my true feelings to my congregation. They look up to me, and if they knew I was like any other man they would demand a new minister in the pulpit."

I understood. I also knew he would be a lot better off confessing his faults than being caught in them. "Has it ever occurred to you," I said, "that what your congregation wants, most of all, is an honest man in the pulpit—rather than a perfect man? The reason you have to turn to someone outside your parish for solace is you are afraid that your own church members won't love you unless you wear your mask. I believe they would love you more if you stopped trying to act pious and started acting like a man—a man who, like them, is searching for the truth."

He was unable to receive what I said. He departed, shaking his head and saying, "You just don't know my people. They demand perfection."

I am convinced the Holy Spirit works best through

transparent persons. In fact, the only way the world can actually see Jesus Christ within us is when we rip off all the masks of hypocrisy, all the veneer of pride, and expose ourselves for what we are. Then, and only then, can the living Christ be seen in us. Until then all we present is an image—and a badly distorted one at that.

Our neighbor told my wife that it wasn't until her husband came home one evening and admitted to her and the children that he was a phony, that they began to find happiness in their marriage. You see, they had known all along he was a fraud, but he couldn't receive their love—or their help—until he admitted his condition.

The best way to disarm a critic is to confess ahead of time. I mean, how can you argue with a man who says he is wrong? Men like this no longer have to wear masks. They are free.

80. *Put on the Whole Armor of God*

For years I was a slave to a strawberry shortcake. While some people have their problems with alcohol, and others with drugs, my problem came the moment I stepped into the cafeteria line at Morrisons and saw one of those big, juicy things beckoning at me from under the glass behind the counter.

Resolutions to stop eating did no more than stir up the gluttony demon which had been with me since I drew my first hungry suck of milk from my mother. I described myself as "stocky," but truthfully I was fat. Blubbery fat. I did everything I knew to get it off. Nothing worked.

I went on a grapefruit diet. I lost twenty pounds in the first two weeks, but my blood pressure went up forty notches and I shouted at my wife, slammed doors behind the children, and kicked the dog. On top of that, I prowled the house at night, looking for cookies, cheese, and candy bars like a drunk looks for a hidden bottle of wine under the sofa cushions.

THE LAST WORD

One night I opened a drawer and right before my eyes was a Hershey bar. I glanced around, saw nobody had seen me, and quickly closed the drawer—my mouth watering wildly. I planned to come back after dark and eat it up. An hour later, after the childen were in bed, I returned. The candy was gone! I woke the entire family when I slammed the drawer shut at one hundred miles an hour, catching the tip of my left index finger in the crack.

The outcome of that particular diet was a gain of eight pounds, backing up the statement of my physician brother who says: "A diet is a torturous period that precedes an increase of weight."

I took up jogging. If you jog in the afternoon you're subject to neighborhood ridicule, so I tried jogging in the early morning. The first morning out I was chased by a huge, brown dog with bloodshot eyes and toenails that went "clickety-click" on the concrete behind me. I sprinted two miles through the subdivision, losing four pounds. However, what I gained physically that morning, I lost emotionally and was unable to speak clearly for five days. In fact, even today when I see a large brown dog with bloodshot eyes, I begin to pant.

The next time I went out was under cover of night. Jogging down a back alley, I paused to gulp some air and heard a shrill scream from a nearby house. "There he is, Howard. I told you somebody was out there." I heard a back screen door slam and what sounded distinctly like somebody cocking a shotgun. It was windsprints home again, accompanied by a twisted ankle when I vaulted a chain-link fence. Despite the fact my friend Costa Deir jogs six miles every morning, I gave it up as a bad try.

"Your brother, who is five years older than you, does one hundred push-ups each morning," my mother bragged. Well, I've had to fight that specter all my life, so I got the Royal Canadian Air Force list of calisthenics and got to work.

The first morning, grunting and sweating in my pajamas, I

jumped and bounced between the bed and chest of drawers. I heard a squeal behind me and turned to see one of my teenage daughters with her hand over her mouth. "It bounces just like jelly, daddy," Bonnie giggled. That sent me to the bathroom to finish my exercises behind closed doors.

Nothing worked, however. I would go on a three-day fast and gain two pounds. It looked like I was doomed to being fat. I knew the issue was critical when the clothing store clerk laughed in my face when I said I wore a size 38 skivvy. Another clerk even had the audacity to say, "Sir, if you'll stop holding your breath I can get a correct measurement."

It wasn't until I got serious enough to realize my problem was spiritual, rather than physical, that the fat began to gradually disappear. It seemed my motives had something to do with it. Sometimes I wanted to lose weight so I would be attractive to certain people. At other times I was motivated because I was going to make a TV appearance. Sometimes I was just plain disgusted with myself—all that shortness of breath and never being able to get in that favorite pair of trousers. It wasn't until I began to realize my body was the temple of the Holy Spirit—and covering it with flab was just as blasphemous as writing obscenities on the wall of the church—that I began to see myself the way God saw me. Sure, He loved me—fat and all. But He made me to be created in His image. And somehow I just couldn't picture Jesus with a potbelly—any more than I could picture Him with a cigar in His mouth.

A friend of mine—a skinny friend, of course—used to say there was something spiritually haywire about a fat Christian. I agree. And with God's help, and for His glory, I'm going to look like him. No double chin and no spare tire.

In the meantime, I give special thanks for a God who loves all the fatties of the world.

81. *The Lighthouse*

Once upon a time, long years ago, I read of a dangerous seacoast where shipwrecks often occurred. Seeing the need, some of the people along the shore built a crude little lifesaving station. The building was only a hut of bamboo poles and palm thatch roof. They had but one boat, a battered old dinghy with rusted oarlocks and two life jackets. The only expensive item was a large incandescent light erected on a pole to give hope to floundering survivors.

The lifesavers were deeply committed to their task. They covenanted together to put lifesaving before anything else. Any who had seen the bloated bodies washed up on the shore knew how critical the task was. With no thought of themselves, they kept constant watch over the sea, going out day and night in tireless search for the lost.

The situation was made more tragic when it was discovered that most of the ships going on the rocks had been chartered by the big Inland Club—a group which had at one time been a lifesaving station before the hurricanes forced it inland to safer ground.

The story is that many lives were saved by this wonderful little band of people who manned the lifesaving station. Many of those saved refused to return to the Inland Club. All they had, they said, they owed to those who had plucked them from the raging sea. They remained on the rugged shore, giving their money and begging the lifesavers to train them that they, too, might save lives. The station grew and the leaders of the band became famous, traveling abroad and teaching others the techniques of saving lives. Since many wanted to become a part of the original group, they formed a loose-knit network of lifesaving groups all over the nation—each looking to the home station for supervision.

Then a great argument arose concerning techniques. Some said the band should not be organized under leaders, but each lifesaver should walk the shore as he pleased. Others felt the lifesaving station was the last hope for those in peril on the sea, since the Inland Club was obviously not interested. Indeed, they were part of the problem. Still a third group insisted on a big, comfortable building like the Inland Club. It would provide refuge for those saved from the sea and give the band a feeling of security and respectability. Finally, there were those who said the whole principle of lifesaving was wrong. If the Inland Clubbers were foolish enough to go out in a storm, they deserved to drown. The Band (now spelled with a capital letter) should be limited only to those who were committed to the Lifesavers (also capitalized).

The group was ready to divide. A large segment felt it was too expensive to maintain the incandescent light on the tower. The lights along the shore were enough, they maintained—citing the words from the old hymn, *Let the Lower Lights Be Burning*.

The Lighthouse

The division was friendly, but final. The *Incandescents* (their newsletter carried the picture of a lighthouse) would continue to meet on Sunday. The *Lower Lighters* (their newsletter had a picture of Jesus standing at the door with a lamp in His hand) would meet on Saturday night. It made them feel spiritual to give way to their self-righteous brothers.

The *Incandescents*, who had more money, built a beautiful lighthouse on the site of the old hut. It had a spacious club room on the ground floor which they rented to the *Lower Lighters* on Saturday night.

As the battle between the groups raged, each side became more defensive. Fewer and fewer members were interested in going on lifesaving missions, preferring to spend their time correcting the other members of the Band. Disgruntled members returned to the Inland Club, declaring the Band had grown legalistic. The Lifesavers, they said, were insisting the members could not go on vacation during the monsoon season and were even demanding financial accountings from some who were slothful in paying their dues. Lifeboat crews had been hired to do the actual work of plucking the lost from the sea, which enabled the Lifesavers time to travel around the country teaching techniques.

About this time a large ship was wrecked off the coast and the hired crews brought in loads of cold, wet, half-drowned people. A great debate arose whether these outsiders should be allowed to enter the clubhouse since they had not made commitments to the Livesavers—who were all in New Zealand teaching techniques. During the debate many of the survivors died from exposure.

At the next meeting the Band divided. The *Lower Lighters* pulled out, insisting their primary purpose was to save lives, not just maintain the lighthouse and keep the bulb burning. They agreed among themselves to go down the coast and start their own lifesaving station. They had done it before, they could do it again.

THE LAST WORD

As the years went by, I understand, the new station slowly went through the same changes that had occurred in the old. A huge lighthouse was built with clubrooms, bowling alley, bingo parlor, and paneled study for the Lifesavers. The committed ones finally pulled out and started another station down the coast. Now, they tell me, if you visit that coast you will find a number of lighthouses along the shore—all calling themselves Lifesaving Stations.

Shipwrecks are frequent in those waters; but most of the people drown.

82. Strangers for Breakfast

Well, it finally happened. A whole family of total strangers showed up for Sunday breakfast at our house. Actually they weren't total strangers, for somewhere I had met them and issued one of those general invitations that no one ever responds to: "If you're ever in Florida, drop in and see us."

They did.

We had flown in late the night before and agreed we'd skip breakfast, get up in time for church, and then eat a big lunch—plans which completely evaporated when the phone rang incessantly at 7:00 A.M.

Last year, Jackie had insisted we put the phone on her side of the bed. If it rang in the middle of the night, she would take care of the questioners without waking me—since I always seem to need more sleep than I get. It was a great idea, only she never answered it. Once asleep she becomes like the tree planted by the waters—she will not be moved. As the phone rang and rang, I crawled over her immovable body and fumbled for the receiver.

I'm always afraid I might have lost my voice during the night, so I practice talking before I pick up the receiver.

"Ah . . . (cough, cough) . . . hello . . . (cough, gag, sputter) . . . hello." Assured I could speak I finally grabbed the cord on the receiver and pulled it to me, over the slumbering tree, and onto my pillow.

"We're here!" a man's chipper voice sang out on the other end of the line. "We've driven all night from Kansas and we're pooped."

Somehow, in my muddled mind, I had a feeling I had made a mistake in answering the phone. "Ah . . . that's nice," I stammered.

Jackie, lying under my shoulder with my elbow in her face, decided to come alive. "You're crushing me," she moaned, struggling. "Who's on the phone?"

"Shh," I said. "They're here. They've driven all night from Kansas and they're pooped."

I could feel her stiffen. "Who's 'they' and how many of 'them' are there?"

By this time I had my hand over the mouthpiece and was trying to get the cord untangled from her hair rollers. "Uh, how many do you have with you?" I asked.

He laughed. "The whole family, of course. Don't you remember saying to bring the gang and come on down?"

"Oh, sure," I said with a fakey laugh. "Let me give you directions. We can hardly wait."

I hung up and fell back on the pillow. "Who was that?" Jackie demanded, now sitting straight up in bed.

"It wasn't anybody. It was a dream," I mumbled.

"Dream nothing," she retorted, squirming out of bed and pulling the covers off me. "You just invited someone to our house at seven o'clock and you don't even know who it is. This place is a wreck. We haven't even unpacked our suitcases. You get the kids up and I'll start on the bathrooms."

Five minutes later the doorbell was ringing. There they were—all five of them. They hugged us, put the kids to sleep on the front-room sofas, and headed for the bathrooms.

I helped Jackie with breakfast while they took showers. "How are we going to learn their names?" she said, as she scrambled through the cupboard for some powdered milk. (We're always out of whole milk when company comes, it seems.)

"I'm going to disappear upstairs and shave," I said. "Since you've never met them, you get their names and when I come back down make a deliberate point of calling their names in front of me."

I started up the stairs and then had a horrible thought. "What if it was you who invited them, not me?"

Jackie chased me up the stairs. "My weakness is screaming at the children," she said. "Yours is inviting strangers to drop by if they're in Florida."

She was right, of course. I should have known that sooner or later someone would take that trite phrase of mine seriously.

"Maybe they're relatives," my teenage daughter giggled while I shaved.

"No, relatives don't call first. They just show up. Let's just pray they're not Bonnie and Clyde."

They weren't. In fact, after Jackie called on the man to ask the blessing at breakfast, I actually remembered where I had met them. Of course, we still didn't know their last names, but my enterprising wife had an answer for that, too. She got them to sign the guest book—just to make sure they weren't angels unawares.

After church our new friends drove on to Miami. This time though it was my wife who waved them on their way saying, "If you've ever back in Florida . . . ."